THE RETAIL JUNGLE

Tales of Adventure and Strategies
to Assist You in Becoming
a Professional Guide

Keep Selling!

J T LaPlante, ABOM

Wasteland Press
Shelbyville, KY USA
www.wastelandpress.net

The Retail Jungle:
Tales of Adventure and Strategies to Assist
You in Becoming a Professional Guide
by J T LaPlante, ABOM

Copyright © 2010 J T LaPlante
ALL RIGHTS RESERVED

First Printing – February 2010
ISBN: 978-1-60047-415-6

NO PART OF THIS BOOK MAY BE REPRODUCED IN ANY FORM, BY PHOTOCOPYING OR BY ANY ELECTRONIC OR MECHANICAL MEANS, INCLUDING INFORMATION STORAGE OR RETRIEVAL SYSTEMS, WITHOUT PERMISSION IN WRITING FROM THE COPYRIGHT OWNER/AUTHOR

Printed in the U.S.A.

Thank You

I have many people to thank for their assistance and support in producing this book, but two deserve special recognition;

*Mr. Ed DeRosa who knows horses;
And is willing to gamble on the occasional long shot,
&
Ms. Nicki Harper of HarperCo – my Editor, now friend.*

Dedication

To my Father, Eugene
(Who taught me how to tell a story)
&
To my Wife, Jennifer
(Who loves me enough to listen)

TABLE OF CONTENTS

Introduction   1

Chapter 1 – I Am a Guide   4
Chapter 2 – Sales Is Simple?!?   11
Chapter 3 – Donate, Don't Front   14
Chapter 4 – Lessons from the Lumberyard   19
Chapter 5 – Why Call It a Jungle?   25
Chapter 6 – Encounter with a Clerk   31
Chapter 7 – Encounter with a Guide   37
Chapter 8 – When a Bargain is Not a Bargain   44
Chapter 9 – Meanwhile, Back in the Jungle   55
Chapter 10 – Sales IS Sales   60
Chapter 11 – The One-Hundred Percent Experience   71
Chapter 12 – Someone Will Buy   81
Chapter 13 – To Guide or Not To Guide   89
Chapter 14 – Jacob and His Miracle   98
Chapter 15 – Of Wants and Needs   107
Chapter 16 – Training the Guides   124
Chapter 17 – Price, Service, Image   131
Chapter 18 – Improving Image   136
Chapter 19 – Service: Rules of the Tour   143
Chapter 20 – Everyone On Board?   155
Chapter 21 – Price or Value   159
Chapter 22 – Overcoming Price Objections   170

Epilogue   179

End Note: Kirk's Mother's Crumb Cake   181

INTRODUCTION

For many years I was a *Professional Guide* through the *Retail Jungle*. After working retail for twenty years in different capacities, I feel justified in calling it a *Jungle*.

Guide describes well my approach to sales. My customers were, to me, *Tourists,* travelers in need of assistance, exploring and searching retail territories in hope of adventure and treasure. I was the *Expert* with the knowledge and experience to help them through the Jungle.

They expected me to have all the information necessary to assist them on their safari. It would be my job to offer my advice, steer them toward good situations and away from bad ones and get them safely to their final destination - a satisfying purchase. In the end, they paid me for my services.

That's a Guide. That's me. And once I decided it was going to be my chosen career, I wanted to learn to be the best at it. That's when it changed from just a ***job*** to a ***profession*** for me. In short, I then became a *Professional Guide.*

Being a Professional Guide turned out to be a great choice because I ended up acquiring the knowledge, experience and savvy to be able to handle almost any requests from those who hired me and the confidence to tackle any new challenges that arose along the way.

Sadly, I'm no longer an active Professional Sales Guide.

I now spend my days lecturing about my adventures, the lessons I've learned, my close encounters with all manner of obstacles and how I overcame adversity at each turn. I've become a *Professional Sales Training Guide.*

Since I've started lecturing, my necessary forays into Sales Jungles now more likely find me playing the role of Tourist. It's been another learning experience for me. I've had to learn to relax and enjoy the Tours given by other Guides, trusting in their ability to help me reach my final destination through their Jungles and safely return home purchases in hand.

Funny though, when I decided early on to be a Professional Sales Guide, the heart of the Retail Jungle is where I thought I'd spend the rest of my life, not burning hundreds of hours a year flying at thirty-five thousand feet; riding in taxis or waiting for shuttles; sleeping night upon night in distant hotel rooms and spending so much time away from those I love.

You see, being home at night and having the time for a life outside of work is the primary reason many of us choose to work the Retail Jungle in the first place.

And discounts - a surprising number of Guides get into the business simply for seasonal discounts. I've always found that weird. Why wouldn't you just look for a sale or clip a coupon? What are you going to do if the next thing you want is a nose job? Run out and try to get a job at a plastic surgeon's office?

Becoming a Guide shouldn't be about saving yourself an extra twenty-seven dollars at *Crockery-Barn*™ for Chanukah. Tourists are counting on you to lead them through your Jungle safely.

Your job as a Guide is to help them avoid pitfalls; explain interesting flora and fauna and expound on local history, traditions and customs, and detail new paths and stops which may have been discovered since their last Tour.

At the end of the Tour, if you lead them through your Jungle without incident, not only will they *pay* you, but they will pay you happily, thank you sincerely and tell others about their Guide and their amazing Jungle adventure.

Because of all this, I ***loved*** being a Professional Sales Guide, assisting those who needed my help in traversing **the Retail Jungle.**

Nowadays, I travel to share what I've learned about the Retail Jungle and how to guide Tourists on successful safaris. Because my audiences asked me to, I've captured my best lessons on guiding for this book.

I'll tell you about the pitfalls that lurk in the Retail Jungle, paths that lead to wondrous experiences for you and your Tourists, routes to avoid that can mire both of you - and I'll regale you with tales of my own adventures.

If you're ready to start, let's take a breath.

Pause, for just a moment....

And now we can begin.

CHAPTER ONE
I Am a Guide

Becoming a Professional Guide wasn't even on my radar as a kid. When I was growing up I wanted to be a dog.

From a child's point of view it appeared to be a pretty good job. My dog played all the time. He got his belly scratched and his ears rubbed. He even got treats pretty much whenever he made the effort to go to the pantry where the treats were stored and make that dog face - you know the one, eyes up, head tilted, and one ear off to the side. (`"What's wrong, fella? You want a cookie? Good boy!"`) His summer days were spent lying in the pooled sunshine on our cool kitchen floor and on winter nights he snuggled on my bed until he drifted off.

It wasn't until my brother burst my dreams at the tender age of four that I started looking for another career path.

It was on a Sunday at my grandparents' house. Dad and Gramps were in the family room watching the afternoon game. Mom and Grandma were working in the kitchen trying to decide if the Sunday night chicken should be served roasted with stuffing, or cut up and baked with mashed potatoes on the side. Mom was championing the former because most of us liked roasted chicken and stuffing. Grandma was pushing for the latter because Gramps liked *Shake-N'-Cook with Italian Herbs©*.

Like most disagreements, it was never only about what is currently being debated, but rather about some deeper, darker subtext which was not being openly discussed. The unspoken resistance here was not to how the chicken should be cooked, but to the accompanying side dishes and specifically to Grandma's insistence on adding boiled rutabaga to every batch of mashed potatoes. This addition usually caused us all to gag.

Even Prince, our Sheltie, who I once saw happily eat a fresh cat turd from a litter box, would turn up his nose at mashed rutabaga-potatoes as if to say, "No, that just ain't right."

Nobody ever came right out and told Grandma that we hated the flavor of rutabaga, out of respect. She had grown up during The Great Depression when they learned to add mashed turnips or rutabaga from the garden to stretch potatoes.

My father had been forced to simply accept the flavor over his lifetime, never knowing the joy of pure potato-dom. My sister, brother, dog and I were having nothing to do with it, since The Great Depression had now been over for quite some time.

Mom was on our side, and hence the weekly debate of Roasted Vs. Baked - a surface-level discussion of adult background static my sister and brother had long since learned to ignore continued, occasionally punctuated by Dad's "Go Packers!" from the other room.

Personally, I always found this ongoing tug-o'-war between Mother and Grandma interesting and couldn't understand why no one had simply suggested to both women that we have baked chicken with rice, baked potatoes or pasta as a side dish and end the matter peacefully forever. But the menu appeared to have been cast in stone by some ancient family agreement before I was around. If the chicken got roasted, we got stuffing; if it got baked, then rutabaga-mashed-potatoes were inevitable.

Yet my sister, brother and I harbored no ill will toward Grandma over her rutabaga-ish tendencies, since other than those awful mashed potatoes she was a fantastic cook.

While all this was happening my brother and I were enjoying an early afternoon snack of ice cold milk and some incredible warm molasses cookies Grandma had pulled out of the oven just minutes ago.

```
That was back when whole milk was the only
way to go and as kids growing up in a dairy
state; "2% milk" would have meant that you had
```

added `98% Hershel's Chocolate Syrup©` to what was in your glass.

It was during a lull in the milk and cookie frenzy that I decided to float the idea of possible future occupations around the room.

"When I grow up," I said, declaring my career choice for the first time out loud, "I'm going to be a dog."

"You can't be a dog," my brother replied with a mouthful of molasses cookie and that you-are-an-idiot look on his face. "You're a person. Only dogs can be dogs. You'll never be a dog."

My life dreams were instantly shattered. I thought I'd nailed it with dog. The only option was to move to the secondary profession on my list.

If a person I must remain, my sights quickly fell on the occupation of grandpa, because from what I could gather at four, it appeared to be the closest human occupation to dog.

Grandpa got to sleep a lot, got a lot of attention from the family by way of hugs and also got a treat almost every time he went to the kitchen. (`"Ed, are you hungry? Let me get you something."`)

I announced my alternate choice during the third cookie, hoping by the lag in conversation to prove I had given this a lot of additional thought and wasn't foolish enough to attempt to choose a path in life without a back-up plan.

"You can't just **be a grandpa**. You have to go to school, then get a job," said my brother trying to explain, as an intelligent thirteen-year old, the complicated idiosyncrasies of employment, finance and household dynamics to a four-year-old child, all the while becoming slightly annoyed that I was bothering him with occupational banter while there were warm cookies to be eaten.

"You mean like Dad?" I asked.

"Yes, like Dad."

"But he hardly *ever* gets to take naps, except on Sundays in church."

The honesty and intricate logic of four-year-olds is often wasted on older siblings.

"And Mom says he can't have cookies because he's starting to look like he's got `Dunlop Disease`," I added in a very serious whisper.

At the time I didn't know what Dunlop Disease was, I only knew it seemed serious and it meant cookies were not allowed, like Grandpa with his *dryer-beet-trees*. Years later, I came to understand that Dunlop Disease meant my Father was getting a little pudgy and Mom was trying to help him get his weight under control. Dunlop Disease was a way of saying that your stomach was reaching a point where it `Dun-lop over your belt` and you might want to steer away from the snacks, especially molasses cookies.

Well, there went my entire list of two. I had honestly thought that at least one of those would provide sufficient socio-economic support for my existence. I mean, if you can't aspire to be a dog or a grandpa as a profession, what kind of world was this, anyway?

I decided to gather some information and take some advice, hoping to refill my list with proper, viable, choices.

"What are you going to be?" I asked my brother, knowing at four that older brothers are wise, pragmatic and, having been in most situations years before you, already have figured out the correct answers to the mysteries of life.

"Fireman or policeman," he said while chewing slowly and looking off into the distance as if able to see the future, "or maybe a baseball player."

OK, three new choices to add. My list was up to three! Grasping the concept now, I tried for four, thereby doubling the length of my previous list and assuring that I had ample choices available to assure fiduciary success.

I turned my attention back to him and asked, "But what about being a truck driver like Dad?" It didn't sound like fun to me, what with the no naps, no snacks thing, but I was curious to know if my big brother had examined this option.

My father was a Teamster, a short-range truck driver, which meant he left for work most days by five in the morning and returned some nights as late as midnight. I couldn't imagine that as a job. Even at four I grasped that it was hard work; but naps or not, cookies or not, maybe this was an option I should keep on the list as a last resort.

At that very second I looked up to see my father who happened to be walking through the kitchen. Obviously it was half-time and he had smelled the fresh-baked cookies for too long.

Mom was cutting up the chicken, and Grandma was starting the pot with the potatoes and rutabagas to boil. (`Grandma one, Mom zero tonight. Yuck! Better grab another cookie while I still could.`) Their backs were turned, so they didn't see him as his hand snaked out, snatched a cookie from our dwindling pile and silently popped the entire thing in his mouth so neither of the two women would detect his pilferage. Seems he had been waiting just outside the kitchen for this moment when both of their backs were turned to make his move, and so was in a position to overhear the conversation between his boys for the past few minutes.

"Jeffrey, don't you ever think of being a truck driver. You can be anything you want in this world if you try; but promise me you won't ever be a truck driver," he said to me with one of the most earnest and serious looks I can ever remember on his face.

"I promise, Dad," I said, and he rubbed my head with a big hand.

Again, with this new promise made, my options appeared to be dwindling as I reviewed the updated career list.

Mom had told me never to go near fires which punched a hole in the fireman route. I was afraid of policemen and they always seemed to get shot in the comic books I had read, so even at four this profession didn't appeal to my better judgment.

Apparently I wasn't much good at baseball either, which I suddenly remembered as I felt a small aching knot on my forehead. My heart was great, but at age four my skills hadn't yet developed. The knot was the result of being too slow in catching my brother's "whizzer express" pitch earlier that morning.

"Put your sights on something fun," said Dad, examining the bump. He heard the game return from commercial and darted back to the living room, but not before giving my brother and me a smile as he snatched the last remaining cookie. He was caught in the act and a chorus of "Eugene!" from Mom and Grandma followed him as he left.

"Maybe you should be a *Professional Dork*!" concluded my brother with a huge smile.

I was less than thrilled with my brother's suggestion. Titles tend to stick with a person; they describe us in a manner which either empowers or hinders us by their sociological reference to our status, position or purpose. Even at four I perceived Dork as being the type of moniker I might want to avoid, professional status or not.

Over the years I've held many titles and have been referenced by many names from family, friends and employers. In addition to Dork, I've been called a Clerk, a Retail Associate and a Salesperson, but none of those titles were actually any more appealing than Dork.

To me, a Clerk has always been someone who just *fills a request*.

Customer: `"Can you hand me that jar of `*`Munson's Knee Ointment`*`© from the top shelf?"`

Clerk: `"Here you go, sir."`

Helpful but perfunctory, that's a Clerk; I would be bored out of my mind if that was all I ever did each day.

There are crude jokes about USPS employees *going postal* and shooting up mail rooms. I've never been a postman, and I have only known a few who chose "posting" as a career. But of the few postmen I've had the pleasure to know, each has seemed to be a jovial, level-headed individual who really enjoyed his occupation. I can't imagine any of them losing it on the job.

Of clerks on the other hand, I've known hundreds. They are, to a man, a strange and angry bunch of people.

I even have a hard time **standing** around a person who's chosen Clerk as a lifelong profession because I can picture him at the end of a long clerkish day holding a box-cutter and mumbling:

`"Just one more… Just one more… If just one more person makes me climb up that rickety ladder to the top of those shelves just to get another jar of `*`Munson's Knee Jelly`*`©; I'm going to take this box-cutter and jam it in their eye socket!"`

No, I don't ever want to end up a Clerk. Besides, I have a fear of ladders, box-cutters and tedium.

The title *Retail Associate* sounded pleasing the first time it was used to refer to me. But if you listen to how it's said, it changes meaning. It's one of those phrases like *bowel movement* or *legal agreement* that describes something common, but is never said in a zealously appealing tone. There is always an air of resignation and inevitability.

"There you are, Mr. Johnson. One of our Retail Associates will be along shortly to assist you with your purchase. Thank you for shopping Phillip's House of Laxatives™."

I've never heard that title used in a positive tone by management either. It usually comes out of their mouths the same way the term *colored people* slips out of the mouths of a few elderly adults - as if to say to both groups, "We know who you are; we know what you are; you have your station in life - accept it."

Salesman, Saleswoman or *Salesperson* never bothered me personally, because it described very succinctly what I was hired to do - sell. But, much of the retail I worked over the years revolved around prescription eyeglasses, sunglasses and contact lenses - and for some odd reason if your industry is linked to anything that could be deemed *medical*, people tend to feel the title *Salesman* has a less than professional connotation. Maybe it's having the word *sales* as part of the title? It's obvious that you can't call them just *persons*, but imagine if other occupations were described in the same manner, incorporating something associated with payment process, as *sales-person* obviously does, into the titles:

Doctor becomes *"Insurance-biller-medicine-practitioner."*

Lawyer becomes *"Percentage-of-award-taker-legal-advisor."*

It's accurate, but I can appreciate that, while not changing the end result, it does cheapen the professionalism of the title somewhat.

So I came up with my own title for what I chose to do as a career in sales, and it fits me just fine.

I'm a *Guide*.

CHAPTER TWO
Sales is Simple?!

Happily, my brother's suggestion was thwarted about twelve years later when I got my first taste of formal employment.

I was hired at age sixteen to work after school and on weekends as a warehouse hand in a lumberyard. My job was to stock shelves with boxes of nails and screws; straighten up the bins of paneling and 2X4s; make sure the bathrooms and break rooms were clean and sweep whenever the floor needed sweeping, which turned out to be an ongoing project.

On a really busy Saturday somebody didn't show up and I was instantly promoted to Salesman.

"Hey kid!" someone yelled from the office area, and then I heard him ask another employee under his breath, "What the hell's his name? Oh yeah," he looked right at me this time," Hey Jeff! Come here!"

It was Roger, the head of the warehouse, and he looked frustrated.

"Jeff, can you help out with the customers?" he asked, a look of suspicion on his face. He asked it accentuating the word "can," which made it sound more a mechanical inquiry than a request for assistance.

"You mean help them load their cars?" I asked.

Plywood and lumber is heavy and I had helped people load a few times before. Once loaded we would give them free twine to tie off the lumber and a piece of red plastic bag to stick on the end if the load hung out the back of their vehicle. If we did a good job they would sometimes give us a dollar or two for helping as a tip. I liked tips.

Tips are the whipped cream of life - free and wonderful on your own personal bowl of cherries.

"No, I mean can you take this," Roger shoved an order pad and a pencil in my hands, "and go take some orders? We have twenty people waiting."

My throat cinched up tight. "Ok, I guess." Not only did I not know how to take an order, I didn't know anything about sales and I was skeptical that it was a tip-able duty.

"Don't worry," Roger said, already walking away to handle another issue, "just ask them what they want and write it down. Sales is simple."

Sales is simple?
The entire opinion of ninety-five percent of the world, summed up in the three word grammatical error of a harried supervisor.

Sales is simple.
Over the years I have spoken with countless professionals from all walks of life, people with degrees of higher education who command respect: doctors, lawyers, politicians and business leaders. I have heard them deliver eloquent speeches and great dissertations on subject matters that are earth shaking, revolutionary and wondrous, offering ideas and conclusions that not only shape the world, but bring together thoughts in such a way as to dramatically define truths which were heretofore incomprehensible by the average person. And, I have heard them say things in the next breath that are so completely clueless as to make you think, "Holy hand-baskets! Did your mother drop you as a child?"

`Sales is simple.`

"Roger must be right, though," I said to myself. (You say things to yourself when you're trying to convince yourself to do something you really don't want to do.) "It must be simple, look at all the people who do it."

For the record:

Sales - IS NOT - simple!

But, with no training, I was about to have several quick sales lessons thrust upon me the hard way.

`This was pretty much the same way I was taught to swim - by being heaved into the deep end of a pool with no life jacket and forced to learn, quickly.`

But I had no idea at the time where this would lead me. I was simply told to go write up some orders. I was being told to go be a Clerk. Maybe, if I just would have done as I was told, I would have never become a Guide. But I've always had this interest in helping people when I could, and I guess in the long run it ended up getting the better of me.

I really just wanted to do what I was asked to do.

But sometimes, doors open.

CHAPTER THREE
Donate, Don't Front

For the sake of any person who has never been in a lumberyard, let me give a brief layout. As in most hardware stores, lumber is usually located either outside, or in areas in the back of the store near loading bays or garage doors so customers can drive their trucks right up to the bins for easier loading.

The bins are sized so that lumber - plywood, paneling and so on - can be loaded in the bins by the pallet with a fork-lift.

As a bin empties, the few remaining pieces are removed; a new pallet is placed on the bottom and the extra pieces from the previous pallet are placed back on top of the full pallet. This way, the inventory is *rotated* so every new load of material is under any leftovers from the previous load. The bin appears full and inviting at all times.

It also means that the product on top is usually the most picked-over leavings of all the previous customers.

This is a really common practice in any kind of retail shop, and in some stores is called *fronting product*. It happens all the time in businesses such as grocery stores, and explains why the freshest milk is in the back of the dairy case.

The reason for fronting is simple - get rid of the dregs, or sell the oldest merchandise first by making it the most easily accessible.

As I became a seasoned Professional Guide later in my career, I came to a realization:

Fronting is great for the books, but horrible for the business, unless there's not a noticeable difference between what's left-over and what's replaced.

Here's why:

By constantly fronting, a company inadvertently presents their worst selection, first.

The fronted leftovers are obviously the first thing a customer sees, so they become the first impression of quality, and as an inspiration to a new sale, they have all the appeal of shaking hands after the other guy sneezes.

Add to this the *Cycle of Fronting* and you get a disastrous downward spiral.

The Cycle of Fronting goes like this:

A business buys and displays fifty new widgets. Over a period of time, they sell forty-five, and front the unsold five widgets in the display. (Notice, they are fronting the five that were considered for purchase and discarded as a selection by forty-five customers).

These five remain on display, along with a restocking of forty-five new widgets which refill the display.

After forty more sales, there is a high probability that four of the previous five that were fronted are still unsold. Since forty-five previous customers thought they were unacceptable, why would the next forty who view the display have a different opinion?

The display is now fronting the four worst from round #1 and the six worst from round #2, along with forty new replacements to once again refill the display.

Each time you refill this happens, until you're eventually left with your entire show floor, your shelves and your display areas primarily filled with your worst-selling or inferior-quality products; because the cycle of fronting is in fact a sifting process, removing the best sellers and leaving behind the worst sellers for the next customers.

Ask yourself this question: Have you ever dug behind the old milk to get the fresh milk at a grocery store?

Why?

Because fronting only works if there's no noticeable difference between the front products and the back products. As soon as the grocer stamps freshness dates on the milk jugs, there's a **noticeable** difference to shoppers.

I once heard sage advice on starting a business from some top executives. It goes like this:

If you want to do well in business, find out what others are doing successfully - and then do that yourself.

When it comes to sales, I've applied it this way with great success:

If you want to do well in sales, find out what customers are buying - and offer them more of the same.

If these statements ring true, then you understand the awful truth about *fronting*:

If you want to turn customers off, sift out products that other customers evaluated and found inferior, and present those first to new sales opportunities who come into your shop.

I guess that poses a question, though: "What **should** be done with the leftovers?" - those widgets that have been sifted through the cycle of fronting yet still remain on your shelves.

The best answer I've ever found was in a bakery.

Bakeries understand the problems inherent with fronting on an intimate level, since the key adjective to their sales is displayed proudly in every sign, in every bakery around the world:

"**FRESH** bakery."

Yet *fresh* is such a short-lived word in the bakery business. A few fleeting hours and *fresh* becomes *stale*. Fronting is attempted while viable, but a bakery's whole reputation can be severely tarnished by a few stale rolls or a dry cake.

So what do they do?

Option #1: Use what has lost its initial value to create "added value" for other business opportunities.

Give those day-old cookies free to children to calm and quiet the kids for a few minutes while the parents order the six-dozen potato rolls they want for Sunday's dinner.

Or, donate most that day-old bread to soup kitchens. Then toast the rest into bread crumbs and offer them free to your customers with every purchase. This strategy might seem impractical for other businesses, but is it?

Let's say you run an appliance store. You have a stock of lime-green toasters you don't seem able to sell. All the other toasters in the rainbow of available colors seemed to sell freely, just not the lime-green ones. You can't return them to the manufacturer for credit, and they are just sitting on your display shelves taking up space where could display new toasters.

Give them away.

Yes, it's true, years from now some whacked-out former hippie might come in on a magic mushroom trip just looking for lime-green toasters and you would have made a killing, but until that time hundreds of customers would have looked at them on your shelf and said, *"Who in their right mind would want a lime-green toaster?"*

But if you give those toasters to a shelter, you now look like a Hero-Philanthropist and get all kinds of good talk started about your store **and** you get a tax deduction for the charitable contribution.

Or, simply give them away to the next ten customers who purchase a **microwave.**

Because we all know that microwaves should actually be called the "Cooking Hand of God" for all the food they can miraculously prepare in seconds, but they are completely useless if you just want a plain piece of toast for breakfast.

You will create such great customer appreciation that it far outweighs the profit produced by the random mushroom-induced sale of a sixteen-dollar lime-green toaster.

Or, if you can't stomach a total loss, go for bakery option #2: Deep discounts for day-old bread.

I would like to caution you on this option, even though it's the one to which retailers all love to flock, because as bakeries and seasoned Professional Guides have often found - day-old-bread discounts create day-old-bread customers, and is that who you really want to be attracting to your business?

A day-old-bread customer, or D.O.B.C. as we will call them, is only interested in discounted day-old bread, or its equivalent. Often, they will not purchase non-discounted items, and in the absence of such will quickly take their business wherever they find a new supply of discounted day-old bread.

Similarly, in a retail appliance store, a D.O.B.C. might be attracted by the Deeply Discounted Labor Day Lime-Green Toaster Extravaganza Sale (the D.D.L.D.L.G.T.E.S. as it's affectionately known) at the deeply discounted price of thirteen dollars & twenty-seven cents per toaster (for a limited time only), but the chance that they will want to add the purchase of a full-priced microwave to their deeply discounted toaster purchase is a stretch, even if they realize at that instant that they are suddenly tired of popping popcorn on a stove.

(To explain for those who don't know, the Cooking Hand of God makes <u>awesome</u> popcorn, which proves beyond a doubt that God is probably a late-night movie buff, but not so much a breakfast person. That's why you should always say your prayers at night. There's a better chance he's still up to listen during commercials or intermission.)

Trust me, give away the day-old bread and the toasters that don't sell to customers already making a purchase; your business will win in the long run.

CHAPTER FOUR
Lessons from the Lumberyard

OK, now that you understand the concept of fronting and my beliefs on it, I can get back to my adventures at the lumberyard.

There were several bins in the back of our lumberyard. I had helped rotate stock and refilled the bins, fronting the leftovers after new pallets had been inserted earlier that day.

Since I hadn't yet learned about the foibles of fronting, I didn't know what to expect, but my first customer pre-confirmed the validity of points I've made on fronting and first impressions.

As I approached a man at one of the 2X4 bins, he was swearing and throwing 2X4s in the back of a battered light blue pick-up truck. I heard him angrily mutter to himself as he threw, "I can't believe these are all bowed!"

SLAM! Another 2X4 hit the truck bed. "I've never seen such crappy lumber!"

He was correct, of course. Previous customers had picked through over a hundred 2X4s and left the dozen worst, bent, splintered and crooked 2X4s to be fronted on top of this pile.

"There are better ones over in that bin," I meekly tried to interject and pointed to where we carried more graded lumber in an alternate bin.

I don't know if he heard me. Between his digging and mumbling (which often included obvious commentary about the lumber's relation to "excrement" and an occasional expletive about "the male offspring of some female dog" whenever he got his palm slivered by a rough piece of wood) he finally looked up and asked, "Do you work here?"

Here began my training as a Guide.

Lesson #1 – *You should introduce yourself when you meet someone in a sales situation.*

That first lesson has stuck with me my entire life, yet you would be amazed how often I find Guides who have never learned it.

The most obvious place to see the positive results of remembering it are in a bar or restaurant. Head into your local hangout and you can watch something interesting. Waiters, waitresses, bartenders and staff who make it a point to tell you their name make far more in tips than staff who decide to ignore the idea.

It probably relates to the fact that `familiarity is the first step to a good business relationship.`

When the bill comes at the end of a meal, you feel a little more generous giving tip money to Cindy, than to *Your Helpful Waitress*.

```
Yes, I realize that some people give a
"standard tip." But trust me, when all is said
and done, to get diners to agree to just drop the
entire fifty on the table rather than calculating
forty-six dollars includes an eighteen percent
gratuity - and YES, it's eighteen percent, not
fifteen percent, you cheapskates - just ask
everyone, "Wasn't Cindy nice?"
```

So I apologized, my first lesson quickly learned.

"Sorry. I'm Jeff, and yes, I work here. I'm not usually taking orders, but you looked like you needed some help and Roger, the Supervisor, asked me to come over and help you out. I was saying there are better 2X4s in that bin over there."

He walked over to the second bin, but stopped a few feet shy, looking at the large price sign on the front of bin #2.

"You charge more for straight lumber?" The second bin was marked sixty cents higher per piece than bin #1 where he'd been digging.

"No, these are more because they are kiln-dried."

"What's kiln-dried?"

Lesson #2 – Customers expect you to know what you're talking about.

Luckily, I knew that one answer, and honestly, it was the only thing I knew about lumber at the time, so I was ecstatic about telling him the factoid.

"Regular framing 2X4s are cut from fresh wood timber which has a lot of moisture. After they are cut they air-dry to fifteen to twenty percent water content. As they dry, they tend to warp a little. That's why so many in that bin are a little crooked. Kiln-dried 2x4s are placed in a heated chamber or oven to reduce moisture after they arc cut. They are banded as they dry, so they dry straighter and warp less. Because they only have about twelve percent water left in the wood when they are done, they stay straight."

The guy had this look of astonishment in his eye like he had been granted an audience with Bob Vila.

Without a word, he walked over to his truck and removed all the lumber he had loaded. He then went to bin #2 and started loading 2X4s from that bin into his truck.

"Write me up for fifty of these."

"Yes sir!" (I didn't even have to help him load it! That was almost better than a tip.)

Instead of becoming a Clerk, I had just become an *Amateur Guide*, and like most Amateur Guides I became almost instantly seduced by the power of *Giving the Tour*: offering sales information and having people respect your advice. That day I became King of the 2x4s! Every sale I made was at the kiln-dried bin and I wouldn't accept disobedience from any mere customer when it came to a question of **my lumber**. And I also learned the *Secret of Expertise.*

Every Guide knows this secret, whether they admit it or not. It's actually quite a simple lesson:

Lesson #3 – In a group, the person who knows one fact that no one else knows is immediately perceived and respected as "The Expert."

Imagine a conversation with any two people, offering direction on which road to take to a given destination. You will see, at some point, someone becomes the *Expert*.

"You take Hillsdale Road," said the first guy.

"No, you take McGovern," said the second.

"You should take Hillsdale," the first emphasizes.

"No, he should take McGovern," counters the second.

And here comes the one fact that no one else knows. "McGovern is closed," says the first. "They are putting in a sewer pipe. I tried to go down there this morning and I had to go all the way back and take Hillsdale."

"Oh (exaggerated pause) you should probably take Hillsdale," concedes #2 to the acknowledged expertise of #1.

Bang, **instant Expert**.

This is such a well-known fact that it even transcends boundaries and shows up in the political arena.

In a political debate it's basically the same rule, so I only watch debates to see if someone presents a fact of which the other party is completely unaware. Whether you're a firm Republican or proud Democrat, if you ever see either one of the candidates say, "Huh, I didn't know that," your decision should be pretty clear whom to give your vote, party loyalty or not.

The reason for this has nothing to do with the candidates. There are millions of facts in every election that no one person could possibly know or remember, so I never hold it against the candidates themselves. But a candidate is just a front-person, a figurehead, for their entire support team, staff and advisors. They are the spokesmen for the intelligence and sentiments of their entire political party, and as such, they rely on everybody on their team to get them the correct responses when they need them.

Did you know that most of the time, for those big debates, the candidates have their full support teams typing to them on teleprompters and whispering to them through little ear phones, reminding them of pre-decided-platform answers to all the questions that may arise? They have support members sending bits of info to jar their memory for the answers they need and probably rehearsed earlier. They do this so, to you watching, the candidates don't sound ignorant of the facts and remember their party's positions on key issues.

However, every once in a while you'll see a candidate take an exaggerated pause before answering. That's because a fact from one side popped up that the other side didn't already know or have a prepared answer for, and the support team has to scramble to not only verify the fact, but to then come up with a positional answer.

```
(See, they are not allowed to type or whisper
to their candidate: "Oops! Honestly, we all
didn't know that! We're stumped!")
```

So the only reason I watch debates is to see if that happens. If it does, I immediately decide to vote for the other candidate, since they obviously have the better support team and advisors.

Yet, the secret of expertise has its weird side as well.

Once someone is perceived as the Expert, for some strange reason, it's incorrectly assumed that they know **everything**.

And here I learned my next lesson:

Lesson #4 – All Tourists who seek you out are looking for guidance, but you may never have all the answers.

As a Guide, a big part of your job depends on being able to provide accurate information, but you won't always have it immediately available from memory.

Throughout my first day, everyone I assisted had some sort of question about whatever they were buying. Luckily some were simply about price.

"How much are these nails?" was one which I could quickly find out the answer to, either from the big price book up at the register, or by asking one of the other employees. But sometimes they really needed help with questions about construction or codes, and they expected **me** to be able to provide it. (Can you believe that?)

I made some great sales that day at the kiln-dried 2x4 bin, but I had at least eight customers walk away from me in frustration when I couldn't answer other questions like, "What's the best grade of plywood for outdoor use?" or "Should I use screws or nails to put this siding up?" and several actually left the yard without making a purchase.

I would like to point out that their departures were really significant, because, unlike today's super hardware centers, nobody came out to our location just to look around.

If you drove all the way out to our lumberyard with a truck, you were expecting to put something in it before you left; so for me to do so badly at sales that they would rather leave than even attempt to speak with another employee before departing speaks volumes.

"Maybe there's more to this than Roger thinks," I wondered.

Sales is *simple*?

If it's so simple, then how could I stink at it? I got upset with my own incompetence.

"I can do this, I know it. I just need to be smart about it. It might not be **simple**, but it's got to be **learnable,** I'll bet."

Some of it is...
Some of it isn't...

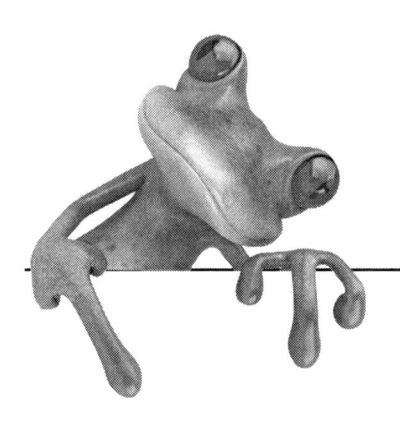

CHAPTER FIVE
Why Call It A Jungle?

I eventually lost the job at the lumberyard, not due to my lack of sales skills, although I wouldn't have blamed them if that had been the reason, but due to general cut-backs. I was part-time and a kid. Everyone else working there was a full-time employee who needed their paychecks to live.

Over the next year I tried a few odd jobs in construction and manufacturing, but I kept feeling as if I had somehow missed my chance in sales and at becoming a Guide.

Still, it was 1978 and life was great. I was living at home with Mom and Dad, but I had my driver's license, my freedom (as much as my parents allowed or knew about), a car and my music, which was fantastic!

If you're too young to remember, that was a great year for music. Disco was peaking, rock was phenomenal and pop was outstanding. Pull up a list of 1978 greatest songs on the Internet, and you will go down the list saying, "classic… classic… classic…"

My only problem was that my stereo had begun to fail. It was a hand-me-down from my brother who believed, as was the fashion of his time, "bigger size means bigger sound" and this was a component behemoth.

Massive floor-standing speakers which had been blasted out by too much high volume playing of the Rolling Stones "Miss You" and Queens "We Will Rock You" Tweeters that could hardly stand up to another straining chorus of "Groove Line" by

Heatwave or "Turn to Stone" by ELO. The cassette heads were almost shot from making copies from my Bob Seger and Steely Dan albums for the car, and the 8-track, (yeah dude - it had an 8-track built in to the tuner) had broken with my Mother's Chuck Mangione tape jammed in it. To this day I can't stop humming "Feels So Good" because it clicked on between every song for eight months.

It was time to upgrade the equipment and downgrade the size for something that would fit in my bedroom and not have to stay in the basement. The term *boom box* wasn't yet fashionable; what I wanted was called a *bookshelf stereo.*

I had saved up four hundred bucks for this system and was ready to purchase.

Where I lived, I had two options for stereo equipment; one was then called *R.D.U. Electronics*™.

In case you haven't figured it out by now, many of these product and location names are altered. I don't know if this place I'm telling this story about is still in business, but if it is, I don't feel like a lawsuit... so as they used to say on the TV show *Dragnot* - the story is true; the names are changed to protect the writer.

However, if you're from the same area of the country as I am, you know this place from their radio ads, which went something like this:

(Announcer's deep excited voice rambling fast and slightly out of breath as he tries to cram a sixty-second spot into thirty seconds of airtime.)

"This weekend only... the Pionair© XLV26 super turntable, belt-drive precision with "close and play" function, you've seen it around for $299 - THIS WEEKEND ONLY $164.17! The Magnavex© RP-184/800 reel-to-reel "dream machine" with the super hi-fi sound booster system, you want it, you need it, you've seen it $288 - THIS WEEKEND ONLY $106.41! (And it always ended with their tag line being thrown in rapidly on the end.) "Get yourself to R.D.U. = P.D.Q.!™"

In other words, it was **the** audio place and known for deals on stereo equipment by everyone.

Alternatively, there was a new electronics *Mega-Store* which had opened recently that people were talking about that I'll call *Circuit Buy*™.

(I was leaning toward *Best City*™ as a store name, but that sounded more like the title of a 1980s songs *J-Tel*© mix album.)

Mega-Stores like *Circuit Buy* were a new concept then.

It's not that a big store was something new to me.

When I was little, we lived in Milwaukee. I got lost one Christmas when Mom and I were shopping at the big Gimbels downtown. Somehow I got on an elevator, and ended up on the wrong floor.

When you're little, everything appears so big and explore-able, and it took thirty minutes for Mom and security to find me. Forty minutes after the search began we were leaving Gimbels.

If you're wondering about the ten minutes between when I was returned to my hysterical mother and our departure from the store, let's just say that talking intelligently to your misbehaving children and time-outs had yet to be invented. Mother had her own method of parental interaction, which involved the careful application of an adult palm to a child's pant-seat.

I don't know the effectiveness rate of the ADD drug, *Ritalon*©; but I do know my mother's method was one-hundred-percent effective in getting the message across and only needed one application; had no harmful pharmacological side effects; was cost effective and produced immediate results.

Today I see parents struggling with the dilemma of using such barbaric methodology when behavioral childhood development issues arise. Let me assure you, in its careful and proper ministration, there is no better lesson you can give a young child than a quick swat on the seat.

Through this method I instantly learned that you do not touch a hot stove; do not play with scissors; do not stray from your Mother in the winter coat department of Gimbels and under no condition **do you ever** play with *Ajinx Cleanser*©, water and a *Brite-o-Pad*© on brand new linoleum no-wax flooring, even if you are a cute four-year-old and it does make "pretty blue swirlies."

The Gimbels incident did, however, physiologically affect my comfort level for shopping in large stores from that day forward. I wasn't hiding. I was seven when it happened and I was glad she found me, even though I got a seat warmer for straying, because I had gotten **lost**! I didn't think that was possible inside a building, yet it had happened.

That incident, probably more than any other, started my thinking of stores as Jungles.

To my mind, if you were in a place where you could get lost among rows, aisles, rooms and floors, separated from your party, and they needed to send hunters out to recover your body and reunite you with your family, then you were in the Jungle.

To this day my opinion hasn't changed, and even as an adult I continually get lost in malls and mega-stores if I don't pay attention.

Have you ever walked through a department store and said to yourself after only a few minutes, "I don't remember which exit I parked by or which doors I entered through?" If you have, congratulate yourself - you too have just gotten semi-lost in the labyrinth of a Retail Jungle. I hope your mom wasn't looking for you, because if she was, you'd better get ready for a time-out, another *Ritalon*© tablet or a ten-minute spanking. (Depending on your family's proclivity, of course.)

Let's get back to my new bookshelf stereo. The proximity of three locations, R.D.U., Circuit Buy and my workplace, was close enough to allow me to choose either one of the stores for a visit during lunch break on Saturday to make my purchase. The clock struck noon and off I went to R.D.U. Electronics.

As I approached R.D.U. from the parking lot and saw the size of the building, all the people entering and exiting, I got a little nervous. But, the advice from every person I spoke with was that "R.D.U. was the place to go" and so my mind was pretty well made up on where I was headed to make my purchase. I needed a new stereo and this was where I was going to buy it, so queasy feelings about the store size or not, there wasn't a choice but to enter this Jungle.

By the way, I love music, it's in my blood. My family is *"artsy"* by heritage. From what I understand Great-Gramps,(Grandma Rutabaga's father), was the branch from which we inherited this tendency. He was multi-talented, having been a noted painter, a famous composer and a talented woodworker. By the time these traits trickled down to my siblings, they were doled out one by one.

My sister inherited the gift of crafts, being able to make anything. She's one of those people who takes a dress pattern and some cloth and actually makes a dress. Give her some pine-cones and a glue gun and you get a wreath that appears store bought. And should you have any extra ribbon, some cloth, a tin can and a piece of construction paper laying around you'll end up with either a Christmas ornament or a recliner.

My brother got the *"artist gene."* Paint, pencil, charcoal or ink, it didn't matter. Animals, landscapes, a still-life or people were all rendered with uncanny accuracy. Add to this his ability to mimic any chosen style - classical, comic book, impressionism, romanticism - and you've got a really talented artist. If he saw it once, he could reproduce it on paper.

Mine is music. I'm no great shakes as a musician. But I **get** music. I appreciate it all, and I understand the dynamics enough that I can work out a tune on any instrument I've ever picked up with just a few hours practice, and I love to listen to it, all day, every day.

These talents aren't exclusive, since all art transcends and interlaces with its sisters. The flow of color is often somewhat musical or rhythmic in a painting; there is an artistic placement of color and texture in a gown or the decorations on a tree and bringing random elements together to create something pleasing to the eye isn't all that different from bringing instruments and notes together to create something pleasurable for the ear.

But the technical-mechanical gene is entirely absent in my family, especially when it comes to electronics.

I've never had a VCR with the time properly set, understood impedance of stereos, and would never have had the enjoyment of hours of *Ybox©* games had they not had the foresight to color-code those three plugs to the corresponding television inputs.

I tell you all this so you can appreciate my arrival at R.D.U. that afternoon. I was entering a Jungle and bound to get lost. I knew that. I was already nervous. I needed a Guide.

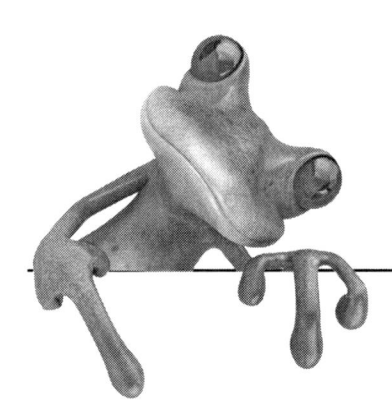

CHAPTER SIX
Encounter with a Clerk

I walked in through the whoosh of sliding doors and realized just how frightening a Jungle I had chosen to explore.

The store was a big open warehouse, concrete floored with industrial steel shelving. The shelving was low enough that you could just see over it, but product on the top shelves often hindered your view from aisle to aisle - hundreds of aisles, thousands of products.

`Help!`

Hundreds of people pushed product-laden shopping carts around while employees rushed here and there to assist. Registers beeped. Boxes were loaded and unloaded. The constant din of raised conversation formed a type of auditory static. People rushed everywhere. But it was also obvious that sales were happening.

"Can you tell me...?" I tried to ask a person, but couldn't get the entire question out of my mouth before being cut off.

"Sorry, sir, I'm helping this customer. Maybe someone in..." he trailed off while walking away, not even giving me complete instructions or a direction. I didn't really blame him. The ratio was probably fifty customers to one employee, and the employees were swamped.

I knew it was fifty to one because you could easily spot the staff by their uniforms - black slacks, white shirts, skinny black ties and a big red plastic name badge with their names in black punch tape.

I always take punch tape names on badges as a sign that employees are frequently replaced, at least so much so that it would be too much bother for the company to make the expenditure on a permanent engraving and thereby take the chance of wasting the funds for a $2.48 name badge if they couldn't hire a new employee named "Claude."

So, with no assistance or direction, I started exploring for myself and I wandered through this Retail Jungle for a good ten minutes looking for some sign of bookshelf stereos.

I saw many employees (black-panted, white-shirted, black-tied, red-tagged), but they were all busier than the one I had met earlier.

I figured my best hope may be to find one by the bookshelf stereos, if I could ever find the aisle with the bookshelf stereos, and eventually I did. My father says, "Even a blind pig occasionally finds a truffle." I admit it was by luck that I found the stereos. They were on the aisle between answering machines and antennas which makes no sense, especially alphabetically. It was a long aisle with three shelves on each side. Both sides were stocked with what appeared to be hundreds of models of bookshelf stereos.

I was here, now if I just **knew** what I **should know** about them to know which I should select, I'd be perfect.

I looked around.

A **Guide**. I need a Guide.

And then, way at the other end of the aisle I saw this kid.

I'm approaching fifty now, so I'm comfortable referring to anyone under twenty-five as a "kid," even though back then he was probably all of three months my junior.

But, there was a problem.
Black pants. Check.
White shirt. Check.
Skinny black tie. Check.
Red badge? Missing.

Now, this predicament only matters if you've ever previously been involved in it. If you have, once is enough, because it's so embarrassing that you'll do anything to avoid it again. It involves going up to someone and asking them for assistance since they appear to be an employee, only to be shot down with that *are-you-an-idiot* look and the exasperated *sorry-but-I-don't-work-here* sarcasm because you've assumed that black pants plus white shirt plus black tie in a store equals store employee.

The first time I made this mistake, the person **did** have on a name badge plus the appropriately colored black-white-black clothing combo. I just wasn't observant enough to notice the badge was black and engraved, and while he didn't know the location of the Worcestershire sauce in the Piggly Wiggly™, he was happy to spend the next two hours attempting to convince me of the validity of attending the Church of Jesus Christ of Latter Day Saints.
I want to make it very clear that I have nothing against Mormons. They are a fine group of people who obviously believe strongly in their religious teachings and can party like there's no tomorrow without any alcohol. This, to me, is an amazing feat. And I would assume once a Mormon, always a Mormon, at least if you're a missionary, since every badge I've seen has had the name engraved, not applied with punch tape.

I wasn't about to make that badge mistake again. In my mind making that mistake was equal to a *shart,* and given the two side by side, I'd rather poop my pants by accident than go through a lecture on my religious affiliation again, so I just looked his way and waited to make eye contact.

We did.
He looked at me, and I looked at him.
He looked at me, and I looked at him.
He looked at me, and I looked at him.
He looked at me, and smiled.
And I thought, "Damn."

Because it was the 80s, and all that "explore the other side" stuff had been going on, and his smile said either "religious," "guide" or "gay," and, facing only a one-in-three chance of success, I figured I was going to have a problem because we were two dudes visually checking each other out for the last five minutes straight.

But he walked over and said, "Hey, can I help you find something?"

Please, I thought, don't add "like salvation."

"Yeah, umm," I didn't know what to call him since he had no name badge and he hadn't offered his name. "I'm looking for one of these bookshelf stereos, any suggestions?"

His first question to me was, "How much did you want to spend?"

That seemed simple enough, straight to the point and logical.

"Four hundred dollars," I said.

Turning and pointing to a system immediately to my right he said, "Then this one would be perfect for you!"

"Why?" I asked.

"It's on sale for $399.95!" he responded happily, seeming pleased with his quick mathematical prowess.

Well, he was right. I gave him some information, and he did his best to follow through using the guidelines I had set. So this needs to be clearly stated, as a Guide, he did nothing wrong, but he also did nothing to assist other than pointing out the obvious.

Maybe he was an *Amateur Guide*, I thought, new to helping Tourists. I still hoped for some as yet unproven assistance and decided to press on.

My first question to him was, "OK. How's the sound on this one?"

He continued to smile, never missing a beat, "Let's find out!"

For the next ten minutes this kid proceeded to push buttons, turn knobs, slide levers, everything he could do to make sound come out of this unit with no effect. (I know what you're thinking. I was too, at first, but he checked the power strip and it was plugged in.)

It turned out that this was one of the first units that didn't use the word "power" on the power button. It was one of those weird

European circle-with-a-line symbols that are now so popular on everyone's computers and appliances. Back then, that symbol was new. Also, the (I guess the proper term would now be the ON button) was on the top of the unit while all the knobs, levers and dials were on the unit's face. As I said, I'm an absolute moron when it comes to electronics, but I had seen that symbol before and I knew that however you describe it - a capital letter "Q" standing on its head, or a clock with one hand stuck at twelve or a zero with an erection - however you name it, you push the button with that symbol on it and the unit turns itself on.

But this kid didn't seem to know that. I was here to buy a stereo, and I was the expert.

"Clerk," I thought, "the kid's an obvious Clerk. He doesn't know any more about stereos than I do. Damn."

The kid was working so intensely with everything on the face of the unit that he never bothered to step back and look anywhere else for a power switch. He was busy. Cassette doors opened and closed, the DVD rack went in and out, every dial and lever on the thing was pinned at *MAX* or *10,* yet there was no music. He did everything but pick it up and shake it.

The longer this went on, the funnier I thought it was, and the less I felt like pointing out to him what I believed might be the button that would turn the unit on and end his frustration.

Finally, he looked at me and said the obvious, "I really don't know much about these things. I just started here yesterday. Let me see if I can find someone to help you."

I tried to explain before he turned away that I needed to be going. (I had only twenty-five minutes left on my lunch hour and I hadn't even eaten). But he had already started to walk off in search of additional assistance.

At this point I simply decided to leave, but as I'm walked away I got this devilish urge, so before he reached the end of the aisle I punched the *ON* button.

It was loud. He had everything pinned on 10, so when it came on it ***CAME ON!*** The entire store silenced as this blasting music came from our aisle.

I quickly walked away, but as I was rounding the corner I snuck a peek back to see the kid desperately trying to find the button to turn the unit off. He never did; he ended up pulling the plug.

That was my experience with R.D.U.

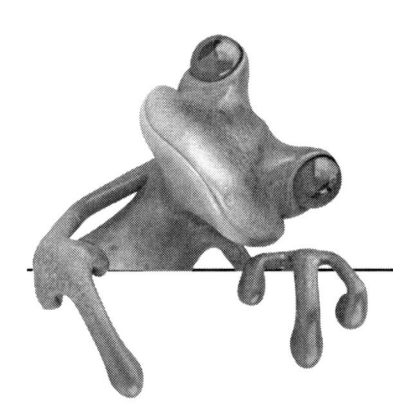

CHAPTER SEVEN
Encounter with a Guide

I wasn't actually thinking about going to Circuit Buy until I realized I had taken the route past their store to get back to work and was standing in front of the building.

Glancing at my watch, I knew lunch was lost today and I wasn't that hungry after my recent disappointing sales experience, so I figured maybe I would just go into Circuit Buy and check out the store to see what all the hubbub was about. I wouldn't buy there, but it would make me feel I had shopped around, even though I was pretty certain that I would end up back at R.D.U. some other day when I had more time and could find someone competent to assist me in my selection. After all, I still believed R.D.U. was the place to get a good deal, and I was on a budget of four hundred dollars.

When I walked through the front doors, I noticed a few differences immediately.

Instead looking like a warehouse, this place was more like a department store. The aisles were wider, and carpeted. The shelves were low enough to allow you to gaze over the entire store, yet held product on the bottom shelves high enough that stooping wasn't required. While still packed with merchandise, this Jungle had the feel of a manicured garden.

The décor said "higher price" and I almost turned on my heels and walked out except that when my toe hit the carpeted flooring inside the sliding doors, three employees turned (one at the Customer Service Desk, one at a register and one obviously already assisting another customer with a purchase) and said to me in unison "Hi! I'll be right with you!"

I was freaked out.

When I was young I watched the Three Stooges© all the time. If you remember their musical "hello" (hello... Hello... HELLO... YE'll-O!), this was the closest thing I've ever heard in real life. I was waiting for someone to quickly yell "jinx!" so the other two greeters would be forced into prolonged silence till someone said their names.

It was that exact, timed, synchronized and verbatim.

I spent the next two stunned minutes just standing by the door waiting for someone else to come in so I could see if it was a fluke, or if they practiced it, but before another entrant arrived the guy who was helping the customer with the previous purchase was available and actually did come over to me as he promised.

"Hi!" he offered his hand, I took it and shook it as you always should when a hand is offered (even before a battle and especially afterwards), gave my name and was informed that his name was Bill.

"Guide," I immediately thought, "this guy's a Guide." He was older, maybe thirty, and looked like he knew electronics. Plus his name badge was engraved - all good signs.

"What can I assist you with today, Jeff?" came the standard opening line. My response was brief.

"Bill, do you know anything about bookshelf stereos?"

"Come on" was his reply and I followed.

There was a smaller selection here. These mega-stores, I found out, often carry a smaller variety of brands, but more different types of merchandise and a larger variety of models from each manufacturer. That wider variety of merchandise, I believe, earns you the privilege of using the title MEGA when referring to your store. There were appliances like refrigerators, washers and dryers as well as stereo equipment. Still, at least a good forty bookshelf stereo units were available here and all neatly arranged.

I opened the sales door a crack for Bill to be certain of his status, ability and prowess as a Guide.

"Any advice?" I asked, viewing the forty available offerings.

His first question to me was: "What did you want it to do?"

Crap! Had I misread it? Was this just a polished Clerk? What do you want it to do and do you want fries with that?

I hoped not.

"What do you mean 'What do I want it to do?' I want it to play music."

"No." He adjusted his posture in a way that said, "This is going to take a while, and we're going to have a good trip, so you might as well relax and get comfortable while I work with you." He paused for just a moment and then he began. "Tell me about yourself." He opened the sales door wide from his side and started his tour. "Tell me about the music you play. Tell me about your favorite bands."

So I told him and he went on, "Tell me about your house, your room," then, "Tell me the layout of the furniture, windows, fixtures." Some of the questions he asked me I couldn't answer, "I, I don't know," and every time I said that he assured me that even no answer was OK.

"What's your favorite radio station?"

"W.S.U.X.," I knew that one.

He also asked me things that I not only couldn't answer, but that I couldn't see for the life of me why they should be asked or answered.

"Do you move a lot? Do you plan on moving in the next year?"

"Now what the heck difference could that make?" I thought, but I answered as best I could.

Finally, after ten minutes of questions, Bill stopped. He took a pause which I would like to say was dramatic, but to me it came across as romantic, because I love to see someone who cherishes his work and does it well, with savvy and finesse. It's why I love to watch golfers address a tee shot then nail the crap out of it. That pause they take before the power of the swing is romantic. Bill's pause was the same.

"Jeff, I think I have two that might be what you're looking for."

TWO? I saw at least five or six below four hundred dollars when we walked up the aisle. I didn't think I'd heard him right.

"Two?" I asked.

"Yes, sir. Would you like to see them?"

I was intrigued to find out why only two, so my answer was simple, "Yes."

OK, this is a **key** point that separates seasoned Professional Guides from Amateurs. Amateur Guides in any sales environment often make the mistake of thinking Tourists want every appropriate suggestion. They don't.

Lesson #5 – All Tourists want from a Professional Guide are a few correct suggestions, which fulfill their immediate needs and are appropriate for their situation, based on the experiences of the Guide.

A Guide might be able to give fifty suggestions (all correct), but giving a Tourist fifty different suggestions is like giving a person lost in a forest a compass and saying, "Just pick a direction and keep going. Eventually you'll find civilization."

Technically that statement may very well be correct, but Professional Guides are usually paid to help make choices easier by narrowing the field.

A Professional Guide's suggestions on directions would be more like this: "If you go north a mile you find a village with hotels, restaurants, and shopping, or, if you go southeast two hundred fifty yards you'll hit a 7-11."

Suggestions like these sure make a decision easier on Tourists and are a mark of a trained Professional Guide.

The mistake of too many options happens all the time with Amateur Restaurant Guides too. (Amateur Restaurant Guide is another term for untrained Wait-staff.

"What's good on the menu? What would you suggest?"

"Everything. Everything is great." (No help whatsoever!)

Bill, as I now suspected, was a true seasoned and trained Professional Guide. He knew two options were all I needed at this time.

He approached the first, which was a beauty.

"Jeff," he said, "This unit does this, this, this, this, this…" On and on and on he went, listing feature after feature.

"Wow!" I didn't know what all those features did, but they sounded important, so I kept my mouth shut.

When he finally stopped he turned to me and smiled, "Do you want to hear it?"

"Hell yeah, I want to hear it!" I couldn't wait to hear how this thing sounded. He had me in the Tour, and I loved it.

Lesson #6 – There is nothing more impressive to a Tourist than a Professional Guide competently doing his job.

Bill turned to the unit and began a choreographed sales dance. He pulled five CDs from his pocket - one jazz, one R&B, one rock, one metal and one classical - and plucked from the group the one I would have chosen. He knew which one I would like, of course, because he had asked me about my music preferences early in our conversation.

He then pulled a cassette tape of some mixed music from his other pocket and put that in cassette deck #1, and then placed an empty cassette in deck #2.

He adjusted the knobs and dials, volume control, equalizers and so on and then tuned the radio to my favorite station.

This last thing I found the most interesting, because W.S.U.X. was a college station most people never heard of and it was way over on the dial. What was even weirder was the fact that I had given only the call letters, not the frequency - and Bill never asked. He simply knew where it was on the dial.

It took him twenty seconds to complete this entire preparation after which he hit the power button (this button actually read POWER - go figure), and absolutely fantastic sounding music came flooding out, not too loud and not too soft.

"Wow!" I started to drool.

Next Bill proceeded to play the CD and the cassette, each equally great. Then he showed me how you could record from radio, CD or cassette to the other deck to make tapes for your car. (Wow!) Next he did a high speed dubbing from tape to tape. (Oh my God, are you kidding?) Then he spent ten minutes showing me every knob, button or dial and explaining all those terms he used to me earlier that I hadn't understood, and told me why each *feature* provided an *advantage* over other systems, and the final *benefit* of these features to me, specifically.

```
Seasoned Professional Guides all know this
sales technique as F.A.B. - features, advantages
and benefits. It is Sales 101. If you're new to
sales and looking for a foothold, learning a
product's features, the advantages they offer and
how these features will eventually benefit the
consumer is an absolute essential to success as a
Guide.
```

Bill even did something extra. He took the stereo off the shelf and showed me every input and output in the back, and told me how they could be used.

Honestly, I never knew you could plug your TV into your stereo before that. Bill was onto the idea of home surround-sound way before it ever became a popular option.

He filled in the gaps. Earlier, when I had been asked questions I didn't understand, I was lost, but now they made sense.

Take the one about "do you move a lot, or plan on moving?" Bill wanted to see how portable I needed the unit to be. Some units may have a better sound because of solid construction, but be heavier to pack. Other units are built more delicately, but could be subject to damage from frequent moving. Still others would be more durable if moved a lot `(or, God forbid, dropped)`, but sacrificed sound quality for durability of construction. Bill was taking all these issues into consideration before making his recommendations to me.

"Wow!" I said, taking it all in.

Out of nowhere another thought hit me. "Hey," I thought, "I'm going to be late getting back to work and I don't even care."

Then it occurred to me. Bill had never even mentioned price. The topic had never come up. I didn't see an obvious price tag, so after a few minutes of just enjoying the music I figured it was up to me to ask.

"Um, how, how, how much is this?" I stammered, realizing that this unit was probably way over my budget.

Bill never wavered, because it was a great unit and probably well worth every penny. He simply said, "This unit is one thousand two hundred and forty."

Lesson #7 – Answer every question from a Tourist directly. Never show angst, fear, hesitation or reluctance over any answer you need to give. As a Professional Guide, your job is not to worry about the facts, simply to present them as they are.

"Dollars?" I don't know why I said that, it just came out.

"We're in America. Pesos would be silly." said Bill, and nothing else.

Professional Guides never balk at giving information, even if it hurts. Bill had sized me up and probably knew this was a lot for me, but it was the best suggestion he had to give me, and he gave his best suggestion first.

This responsibility, of giving your best suggestion first, is another mark of a Professional Guide. It is often referred to in sales as the *top-down selling system* and is the **only** way several sales options or product choices should be offered.

Lesson #8 - The first suggestion of a Professional Guide is the Guide's primary suggestion - and as such, should always be the Guide's best suggestion.

It would be negligent for a Professional Guide to offer an option that would be superior, or better fulfill the Tourist's immediate needs, as a secondary suggestion.

Amateur Guides often succumb and break this rule when faced with resistance from Tourists. That's another measure of a Guide's professionalism - being steadfast to proper suggestions made to a Tourist.

CHAPTER EIGHT
When a Bargain is Not a Bargain

Becoming a Professional Guide isn't only about professionalism; it's also about obtaining and maintaining a high skill level in salesmanship. A good measure of a Guide's skill level is the ability to set sales goals and to consistently achieve required daily, weekly, monthly, quarterly and annual sales targets.

Sales numbers vary - that's life. And brief periods of lower sales happen to everybody in retail. Though it's something to keep your eye on, it's nothing to waste time worrying about unless it becomes prolonged.

When sales drift downward for long periods it's common for inexperienced Amateur Guides to blame failure in reaching sales goals on the customers or the economy. Unfortunately, this usually isn't the case. Prolonged lower-than-average sales are typically the result of a combination of:

- The Guide's own shortcomings in building salesmanship skills or
- A poor effort by the Guide to fully understand the features, advantages and benefits offered by all the products or options they represent, or possibly
- The difficulties which can be precipitated by certain marketing strategies and advertising campaigns adopted by a business.

The first is a basic fact of life; without honed skills it's difficult to perform any task correctly.

The second seems fairly obvious as well. A total understanding of all products and options allows the Guide to represent them competently during the Tour. How can we possibly represent correctly what we ourselves do not take the time or make the effort to understand?

The third reason is a complex and often misunderstood situation, yet those of us in retail having problems with our sales figures love to jump there first rather than face the possibility that the lack of sales could be the result of our own shortcomings. It is used as an excuse by many Amateur Guides for poor sales performance and is often erroneously accepted by managers as a reasonable excuse for lackluster sales because managers, like Amateur Guides, usually have very little influence on the marketing decisions of businesses. They, like their subordinates, accept what appears to be an unavoidable hindrance foisted upon them by the owners or the marketing department, and a logical response for the breakdown in sales is resignation to the philosophy that control of the sale is out of the hands of the sales staff. Usually managers who accept these excuses dig no deeper for the actual cause, such as poor sales skills, and eventually the location crumbles.

Without a comprehension of the business's marketing strategies and the expected issues inherent in most advertising campaigns, Guides can find themselves questioning their own motives for making any suggestions at all, and can eventually revert to becoming Clerks. Bad for business, bad for managers, bad for the Guides.

So, it would be beneficial to take a moment and look at a common advertising campaign that particularly causes trouble for Amateur Guides, and learn how to cope with and compensate for its prevalence in a sales environment.

The advertising campaign? **Low price advertising.**

```
    It's a great example of how what seems like a
promising marketing strategy can work against its
```

own goals if the effects are not understood by everyone involved in the organization.

When management, advertising and a business's market strategy are concentrated on **only** "low price" advertising as a means to attract new customers; certain situations arise:

- Amateur Guides cannot comply with the rule of top-down selling
- Current clientele may be lost
- Guides are put in an awkward position with Tourists

A long term - low price campaign usually stems from a lack of faith by management in one of three sales areas:

- The quality of what is being sold, or
- The salesmanship skills of those hired to sell, or
- An extremely competitive market

Usually, it's the third reason. This seems pretty obvious because if you had great products and skilled sales staff, then sales should fall at an acceptable level for your industry. *(Assuming and accepting the expected customary variances caused by seasonal fluctuations in the market, or variances caused by location and so on.)*

But let's assume you have good products, fair standard prices and relatively skilled sales staff. This leaves only one reason for a low price campaign: you're in an extremely competitive market and you want to build gains based on volume alone.

By promoting low prices, advertisers and marketing departments have found a quick and easy **"cheat"** that appears to draw more customers to a location. It sounds very attractive to any business that wants to see immediate increases in sales volume, but even the business owners themselves often fail to understand the ramifications of accepting this plan as a long-term marketing strategy.

Funny, while detrimental to sales in and of itself, this method of advertising works for the same reason Professional Guides succeed:

Tourists lack information.

Lesson #9 – In the absence of more relevant information, all options appear valid and equal, and the most commonly known variable will be deemed the only measure for comparison. Often, this common variable is <u>price</u>.

But we need to remember that every business has two teams with very different objectives:

- **Sales**, which is the assigned territory and responsibility of Guides, is focused on sales satisfaction **(quality)**.
- **Marketing and Advertising**, which has its own rules, territories and Agents, is focused on draw volume **(quantity)**.

These teams, while attempting to work toward a common goal, often become combative when low prices are the business's long-term marketing strategy; and the focus of Management swings too far from **quality** toward **quantity**.

Here's how the battle plays out.

Higher quantities of Tourists arrive, driven by low price advertising, and Guides proceed as usual, gathering information and attempting to make appropriate product suggestions.

Since the low price items advertised often lack key features required to completely fulfill most Tourists' immediate needs, the Guide's suggestions of higher quality items that are appropriate for the immediate needs of the Tourist are often different from the products or options promoted in the low price advertisements.

When price is eventually discussed, the Tourists begin to complain about the Guide's suggestions since they are not in line with price expectations created by the low price advertising.

Tourists, unfortunately, believe that an advertising *Show (commercials, ads, coupons)* is the same thing as a guided Tour. This is obviously impossible, since there is no way that any advertised suggestion is the correct suggestion for everyone.

Since advertising *Shows* reinforce the assumption that all products are equal and promote the notion that the only variable a Tourist should use in decision making is price, a conflict is bound to happen.

Amateur Guides meeting this resistance feel disheartened, or get worried that they have done something wrong or improper with the Tourist's trust and respect. They begin to place a priority on only satisfying the Tourist's financial goals and eventually turn away from suggesting products or options they know are superior, in favor of quick approval from the Tourists for respecting the low price advertisements of the business.

Since they are not steadfast in their resolve that they are correctly making the appropriate primary suggestions, they falter, second guess themselves, begin to temper their suggestions to more closely match the advertising and become Clerks.

Over time they may totally stop suggesting, and simply begin to fill low price requests, which were created by the low price advertising's effect on uninformed Tourist's minds.

This problem compounds if Amateur Guides do not fully understand all the features, advantages and benefits of the products or options they are suggesting, or why they are important, or what they actually will do for the Tourist, or what will be the result of their absence. Then the Guides can't possibly support their positions or suggestions. Guides need to have faith in themselves and the products or programs they represent. This is why knowledge is such a key element in becoming a competent Professional Guide, and why Professional Guides are generally better equipped to handle price objections.

Now, let's look at what happens to clientele demographics when a store continually relies on adverting only low prices, and how this type of marketing campaign, while having the possibility of drawing a higher volume of new clients, may alienate many others that the business would prefer to interest.

First, let's look at how low price advertising relates to the average consumer demographic.

Low price advertising actually only influences about half of consumers - the half of consumers who fall into the categories of Value Seekers and Deal Makers.

The other half of the market is made up of consumers who are looking for product quality or name brands. These consumers are typically known as Technical Innovators and Brand Loyalists, and they are actually **repulsed** by low price advertising, believing that discounted prices represent lower quality or a lack of brand selection, so they tend to avoid "low price/discount" locations due to the advertising.

This is an ugly secret inherent in long term low price advertising campaigns which is never brought to light by marketing firms or advertising agencies that suggest this tactic.

Second, the customers you gain through low price advertising are the least loyal clients, and will leave your business immediately when they discover a lower cost option. *(Another fact marketing doesn't talk about.)* Remember the D.O.B.C.'s?

Third, to compensate for ongoing sales of high volumes of low price merchandise, management frequently demands that the sales staff "push" alternative higher priced/higher quality options and name brand products on customers whenever possible and "up-sell" the clientele. This high pressure sales technique upsets most of the customers who visit, since they were drawn by the advertising.

Businesses are surprised that they have alienated more profitable consumers by their choice of advertising campaigns, and incorrectly assume they can generate higher-price buying from Value Seekers and Deal Makers who are already predisposed to reject it.

Soon terms such as "loss leader" and "bait and switch" get thrown around by disgruntled consumers who were drawn by the business's low price advertising.

In an attempt to force the scales, some businesses begin hiring unscrupulous snake-oil sales-persons who assuage management's increased dependence on profitable higher ticket sales by *over-selling* without regard to how those sales may or may not suit the client's needs.

Any Professional Guides have long since left these companies, or soon will, if management doesn't try to balance the equation of quantity versus quality.

What a waste! Money spent on advertising to bring a section of the market through your door that likes discounted products, only to hit them with the absolute opposite in selection the moment they talk with someone whom they believe is meant to correctly guide their purchases.

No wonder everyone gets upset. No wonder Amateur Guides give up in frustration and revert to being Clerks.

For these reasons, low price advertising is probably the worst long term strategy a business can adopt **if** it wishes to promote the quality of its products and services, or support the ability of its Guides to be professional and responsible.

As a Professional Guide you cannot allow marketing and advertising campaigns to influence your suggestions of the best products or options to fulfill a Tourist's needs.

The moral of all this is easy. For any business, doing too much low price advertising changes the overall demographic of the clientele. Shift you're demographic to the low end for too long and you will lose not only your best high end clientele, but also your best Professional Guides.

As management, if you feel your sales numbers aren't where they should be, just make sure you have trained Professional Guides working your Jungles.

Professional Guides take responsibility for their sales figures.

Unskilled sales people have a hard time selling, and almost always that's directly attributable to an unjustified empathy for the assumed financial constraints of the customers.

If you're taking a sales position in the hopes of eventually becoming a Professional Guide, and you have a problem with **financial empathy**, you're delusional about your career choice. You simply are not cut out to be a Guide at all. Guides can't afford financial empathy; it means you have a need to justify every sale to yourself and your own financial situation.

How is justification ever possible? In one year I sold over a million and a half dollars of merchandise; that same year, if I'd have attempted to justify what I could personally afford from my personal discretionary funds for the whole year, I would have stopped selling at $17.29.

Financial empathy is one of the only two innate reasons some people should never choose Sales Guide as a career path.

The other reason a person should automatically choose any career other than a Professional Sales Guide is if they have a problem with **intestinal fortitude**, and actually **would** allow marketing, advertising or management to pressure them to push products or options with a total disregard to the immediate needs of Tourists.

We are Professional Guides, not snake-oil salesmen. For most of us, if management suggests we push inappropriately, we generally suggest back to management that they push as well: "Hey, why don't you push yourself up out of that chair and go take a long walk off a short pier?"

BE WARNED: By telling a boss to "take a long walk off a short pier" you will lose your job! But you will also regain your integrity and intestinal fortitude and be a better person for it. You will also be back on your way to becoming a Professional Guide who understands every sale is ultimately down to decisions made by just two people, the Guide and the Tourist.

So, if you feel you **may** actually be in the position of being pushed, **before** you do anything foolish, do some research. You may realize that you are not being told to push something, but are in fact being given a new option and being asked to offer it.

I've known many Guides, Professional and Amateur, who got all worked up over feeling they had been instructed to push one product over another only to find out through research that the product they were instructed to push actually was a better product than the one they were previously suggesting.

Their hard-headedness, ignorance or failure to embrace new products and options caused these people to quit their jobs over nothing. They didn't properly research or embrace the opportunities, features, advantages or benefits presented by newer products and wrongly assumed the reason they were championed by management was solely based on profitability. They left their position over nothing.

An earlier message bears repeating:

Knowledge is a key element in becoming a competent Professional Guide.

A golden rule, to be safe, is simply to follow the next lesson:

Lesson #10 - A Professional Guide never worries about what's advertised, only what is the best for their Tourist's immediate needs, and price should only be an issue if the Tourist brings it up.

You may find this helpful to remember:

You are only a Guide when you're involved with the Tourist in a face-to-face sales situation.

This confuses many people who work in Jungles since they have such a hard time understanding that we all wear different hats throughout the day. Guides want to just be Guides, marketing and advertising agents want to just be marketing and advertising agents and owners want to just be owners. But many times, business forces other hats on each of us.

A really common mistake for Guides is to believe that they are still Guides during most business phone calls.

Phone calls, with the exception of service calls, are the express property of marketing and advertising.

When a customer calls with an inquiry and you pick up the phone, you are not a Guide; you are now a marketing *Agent* and have become a part of your company's advertising campaign.

Think about it. What do marketing campaigns and advertising do? They invite Tourists to visit your Jungle, drawing them in by creating some type of interest.

When a phone rings, if it's not a service call, it's usually someone testing the waters for a Tour. They are still in the mode of building interest, and it's your job at that point, as a temporary marketing agent, to proceed with whatever campaign the company has in place.

This is because marketing and advertising Agents fight something Guides do not - *competition*. Guides never fight competition directly; by the time we begin a Tour it's just us and the Tourist.

Competition is why they developed the low price advertising campaign to begin with, and though it may create issues we will need to overcome on the Tour, as a temporary marketing Agent you are obligated to follow their rules when in their arena.

So, when the phone rings and a Tourist asks, "How much are your widgets?" we always need to answer, "Widgets **start at** five dollars and go up from there," even if we have a pretty good hunch they might need a twenty-dollar widget.

You will hear from many other books and speakers that "you are always selling." That may be true; but Guiding only happens when you're actively on a Tour. When you are on the phone is one of the times you're not an active Guide.

A Professional Guide is only selling when she is directly immersed in the process of gathering, translating and supplying information directly to the Tourist; that's the Tour, and it's what we live for.

CHAPTER NINE
Meanwhile, Back in the Jungle

Back to the story of my Tour of bookshelf stereos, where Bill is gathering, translating and supplying me information directly.

(Unfortunately, what he's supplying isn't helping my immediate situation.)

Price.

I brought it up that day at Circuit Buy. Your darn toot'n I brought it up to Bill; it was an issue. I had a pre-conceived notion that these stereos were all basically the same general price, and I had a budget.

At one thousand two hundred and forty dollars, price was a huge issue.

"Wow," (I apparently said "wow" a lot in the 80s) "I don't think I can afford that. It's more than I wanted to spend."

"Would you like to see the other one I would suggest? It might be closer to your budget," he asked.

"Absolutely!" I replied, relieved.

Bill walked me over to another model, which looked basically the same to me, and he began, "Jeff, this one does this, this and this." Round one all over again. It was another great Tour, only I noticed the list was shorter this time.

He pointed out the omissions, "What is doesn't do is this, this, this, this and this."

Crap! I'm screwed.

See, I would never have missed those features unless I had already experienced them. I understood them, and I started thinking about how they would be cool to have, and now I'd just lost them.

Bill came in without missing a beat, "But this one does do this, this and this, which the other one didn't."

Huh! What do you know about that? I guess I'm going to have to think about this a little.

"Would you like to hear it?"

"You bet!" I said

"Here we go," said Bill

Fiddle, fiddle, fiddle, tweak, tweak, push, slide, and beautiful music flooded the area. Bill showed me all the buttons and knobs, did the full demo, but it went quicker this time because he was training me, and I already understood more than I had ever known.

To be honest, even though I'm musical and have a great ear, this one sounded just as good as the other.

"Wow!" *(Again with the "wow")* "I really can't hear a difference."

"Neither can I," Bill admitted, "and this will save you a lot." He told me the price. Gulp! Eight hundred and ninety-nine dollars. He saw me pale, but said nothing.

Lesson #11 - Great Professional Guide rule; when there's nothing to say - say nothing.

I broke the silence, "I think that might still be more than I think I wanted to spend."

Bill asked me forthright with no offense taken, "OK, Jeff, how much did you think you wanted to spend today?"

I was taken back. What did this guy want to do, see the inside of my checkbook? And then this weird thing happened. Maybe it was because I was in this nice store, or maybe because I felt I was put on the spot, or maybe it was because I didn't want to sound cheap to Bill. I started to say the amount, but kept bumping it while I was saying it.

"I wanted to spend, ah, four, no wait, I mean, five, yeah, five hundred, and uh, ah, fif – no, sev – ah, EIGHTY um eight or nine dollars, around there like somewhere." I trailed off, but Bill rescued me as a true Professional would.

"Jeff, I would love to sell you the perfect stereo for five eighty nine, but I don't have one for that exact price. I've got one for five twenty five that's a good deal, and I've got one for six ninety nine that's marked down to six hundred flat. But I don't think they're right for you."

"Well, can I see them?"

"Of course!" Bill never wavered. He ran the same demos but he was right, they weren't for me. The sound was OK, but that's just it; it was OK - not the beautiful rich tone I had heard from the first two.

Later I realized, had I had never heard those first two sounding so good, I probably would never have thought these two sounded inferior.

Lesson #12 - Guides cannot always expect a Tourist to fully understand or appreciate the full benefit of their professional guidance until the journey has ended.

If you're a Restaurant Guide, you can't expect a Tourist to tell you how much they will enjoy the special before they eat it, especially if it's a dish they've never tried before.

This is why Guides, all Guides, are so critically important. A good Guide can makes suggestions you would never think of for yourself.

This is also why, in a good Guide–Tourist interaction, both parties are pleased. The Tourist is pleased with the good suggestions, and the Guide is pleased to see his services appreciated and his suggestions happily confirmed. This goes beyond the Tour, this has a deeper meaning I wouldn't fully come to comprehend or appreciate for quite some time.

For me, then, Bill's suggestions were spot on, and unlike a meal in a restaurant, he was able to give me a taste, and I had to admit I liked it. Fifteen minutes later I was walking back to work with a stereo.

I ended up getting the one for eight ninety nine and I was happy with my purchase. It was over my budget, but a budget is, for most of us just a suggested self-imposed limit created to provide funding for one project, while protecting funding for another. Don't spend too much over here, so we have some for over there. But people change budgets daily based on circumstance and situation.

Besides, Bill had also thrown in a lime-green toaster. (Just kidding.)

What he had actually thrown in was my first complete Tour experience with a true Professional Guide.

As I reached my job, my boss saw me and started making a big deal of taking a two hour lunch to buy a new stereo, so I quit. I was wrong to be late, but that didn't matter. I had realized that I really wanted to be like Bill. I wanted to help people and make a difference. I wanted to learn to do a *Tour* and that *pause* thing, and I wanted the respect and praise earned by being a Professional Guide.

So I quit, and that night when I went home I played song after song on that stereo and slept like a rock. As I was drifting off, I was looking at my new stereo and I got this strange feeling that I had seen it before. After a few minutes I was certain, I was pretty darn well sure that I has seen this exact same stereo at R.D.U. when I was looking around, and I'm pretty sure they had it for eight hundred seventy-six dollars and fifty-four cents, because I remembered thinking how odd it was that the price was like that, all five numbers of the price descending in a row. All I would have had to do was go back to R.D.U. once more to check it out and I could save twenty bucks.

No, not worth it.

```
    Whenever  I  tell   this   story   I   always  get
asked, "Why didn't you buy the first stereo? If
Bill was that good a Guide, he should have sold
you that unit. Wasn't it his best suggestion?"
    The    answer   is;    it    was    my    decision.   It's
always  the  customer's decision.  In this case the
only  real  difference  between  the  first  system  and
the   one   I   got   was   that   the   first   unit   had  a
remote  control  which,  at  the  time,  I  didn't think
I needed.
    Since  then  I  have  purchased  several  stereos,
and every-one has had a remote control. Honestly,
```

I don't know how I ever did without it, but remember I was young and this was going in my bedroom. I didn't mind getting up to switch the channel or start or stop a tape. All I would have wanted the remote for was turning it off from the bed without getting up when I was tired.

    I solved that problem by making a seven dollar purchase on the way home.

    That night, Clap™! Clap™! and I was asleep and three hundred twenty one dollars ahead.

CHAPTER TEN
Sales IS Sales

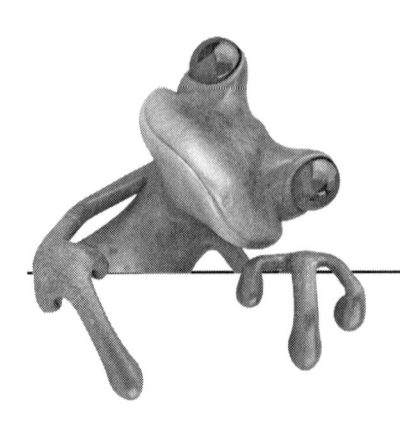

It was a job, it was in sales, and it was a nightmare.

I don't even remember how I got that job, but it was one of those "Do you want to make big $$$? Do you want to be your own boss?" kind of ads, and the next thing I knew, I was selling encyclopedias.

What can I say? I'm like everyone. I know advertisements, commercials and coupons shouldn't really guide you on any decisions, but they do.

I think I took the job because it was offered, and I needed a job and I thought I would be learning about sales, but it was awful.

Basically, people signed up in malls and shopping centers to win a free set of encyclopedias, (or one of several other fabulous grand prizes), only to miss in the microscopic fine print that the odds of winning the encyclopedias or any of the other grand prizes was 1,000,000,000 to 1, and your chance of winning a set of cheap steak knives was 1,000,000,000 to 999,999,999. If you're bad with odds I'll spell it out for you. Everybody got the steak knives.

Now here's the kicker: you didn't know which one you were entitled to receive until you got your prize envelope, which would be delivered by someone (me) only after you agreed to listen to a thirty minute presentation on the encyclopedias (you MAY win), in the comfort of your own home.

"What time can we send our representative by this evening? And of course, you, your wife, and your entire family must all be present."

Yikes. I can't believe people went for this, but they did, by the hundreds.

The company had twenty of us making between two and four calls each during an evening, and they never ran out of appointments.

Territories were assigned by seniority. Seasoned professionals were the Territory Managers, like my boss. They got the homes in the suburbs with school-age children in private or parochial schools.

I was new, so I got the worst, most horrible, dangerous, dark, dank and depressed areas of my fine city, with often-struggling-to-make-ends-meet single parents, laid-off factory workers, or on-again off-again drug addicts and alcoholics.

The homes to which I was sent often lacked all the windows, or were government project buildings covered in graffiti or were small apartments over old taverns or grocery stores.

People passing through these areas of town knew better than to look anyone else directly in the eye, because if you did the difference between them and you was often swiftly pointed out with a tire iron or broken beer bottle.

And here I come, in my polyester navy blue suit, shiny shoes and invitingly large *pleather* (imitation leather) carry tote for the encyclopedias. And what am I bringing these model examples of citizenry?

Six razor-sharp knives!

Nightmare.

And even though this wasn't a retail Jungle, it was a definitely a Jungle and I was expected to be a Guide.

My impetus for staying with this job longer than the first call was hope - hope that somewhere in this mess was a family or two trying to get it together, who actually thought of their children's future before their next bottle of vodka.

Maybe there was a family that understood the value of education, not in making you smarter, but in building a scholastic ladder so your kids can climb up and over this life and be the something better that, while too late for you, might be possible for them.

Encyclopedias might be that ladder. I believed that, so I took this job and found myself as a Guide with a single known path, through a Jungle more hideous and dangerous than a simple retail store.

But it couldn't be that hard, remember;

Sales is simple... isn't it?

As I learned earlier, *sales – IS NOT – simple*. But there's a line which sounds close to that which you may have heard:

Sales – *IS* – Sales

This old chestnut has been an accurate sentiment, for which I've never found contradiction.

All the lessons in this book are universally true, no matter what your Jungle is - retail, wholesale, service or consulting. Throughout these pages I have often referred to different Jungles, or environments, where certain sales techniques are used and the benefits of those lessons more easily spotted.

Yet, as I take you through my experiences selling encyclopedias, I think it's important to understand that some of the situations I faced are unique. For this reason I hesitated to include these stories, but the **basic lessons** I learned are applicable to retail, and will help make you a better Professional Guide, so they had to be included.

Over the years, as I have spoken with many Guides who work a variety of Jungle environments, I came to understand that each and every Jungle has its own particular idiosyncrasies to which a Guide must adapt.

Some Jungles have very specific time constraints, so the talents of the most successful Guides revolve around not only following the lessons in this book, but devising a strategy for handling Tourists within the allotted time.

Some Jungles are easy to maneuver, with few traps and hazards to avoid - like the Pizza Jungle:

Go to any good pizza restaurant and you will be presented a menu with twenty different kinds of pizza, a barrage of topping choices, combos, side dishes. Your Restaurant Guide can be a fantastic asset in getting the most for your money, steering you away from some bad choices and making certain your experience ends on a positive note.

But, even if you end up getting a Clerk who just takes your order, the Pizza Jungle might be a fairly easy one to navigate, given the fact that you, like most people, may have already had a pizza or two in your life and have a bit of your own experience to rely upon in a pinch.

In a sense, this Self-Guiding is what allows us to make purchases of common items without continually requiring Guide services on every purchase.

Eat twenty times from the same pizza parlor and whether you know it or not, you've gained some Pizza-Guide experience of your own!

Still, some Jungles are terribly difficult to maneuver. The harder it is for a Tourist to traverse a Jungle without assistance, the more obvious the benefits provided by a Guide become.

Extremely vast or confusing *Problem Jungles* absolutely require the assistance of a Guide, and sometimes the services of a special category of Guide are required even to enter some Jungles, the **Certified Specialist**.

Certified Specialists sell, but under the auspices of a license. Pharmacies, optical practices, insurance offices and realtors are just some of the businesses that require Certified Specialists.

Still, it is beneficial to point out the obvious truths:

- ```
  Clerks are not Guides
  ```
- ```
  Amateur Guides are not as skilled as seasoned Professional Guides
  ```
- ```
  And, not all Certified Specialists are Professional Guides
  ```

Moral: A license does not a Professional Guide automatically make.

A very visible example of these truths is found in most pharmacies.

My prescriptive needs are few. I believe that prescription medicine is best taken when it's absolutely necessary to cure chronic illness or remove intense pain, so I've only taken
  ```

antibiotics a few times when necessary and used pain medicine, other than aspirin, when I've had broken bones.

But over-the-counter is fair game, and I'm a big fan of preventive therapy like vitamins and supplements.

I use the pharmacy I do now, because of the Guide services of Wendy, a Professional Guide who also happens to be a Certified Pharmacy Specialist. Wendy and I met, as sometimes happens between Guide and Tourist, by accident.

Believing in supplements, I've used them as proper when I'm in a fitness mode. My fitness mode usually follows my holiday mode, which usually follows my visit-the-family mode, which usually follows my vacation mode. Feel free to substitute the word "eating" for "holiday," "family" and "vacation" in the previous sentences. As a matter of fact, my only mode that doesn't directly involve connection to eating in some manner, form or direction, is probably my sleeping mode, since I'm half Italian.

In fitness mode I take L-carnitine and chromium picolinate to speed up my body's ability to burn sugar and turn fat into energy. Chromium picolinate promotes a healthy metabolism by helping the body absorb glucose, the "sugar" in blood sugar, more efficiently so it can be used for energy, and L-carnitine is an amino acid that helps in fat metabolism, transporting long-chain fatty acids into the mitochondria, which act like powerhouses and make energy available to the body of the cell.

```
Tell this "one fact" to anyone who is dieting
and doesn't understand supplements, and you will
find out the rule of expertise works exactly as I
described earlier.
```

I learned about physiology, how calories are burnt and the body's ability to store and release energy, because I owned a sled dog once (long story I'll save for another book) and was trying to figure out how that dog could eat so much and never get fat. Turns out it has to do with huge levels of mitochondria. So I figured, if it works for dogs, it's got to work for people.

Besides, as I grew up I never fully got over that "not allowed to be a dog" career censorship my brother threw on me, so anything that got me closer to dog-dom over the years has seemed acceptable. So, I take chromium and carnitine to shoot for a dog's metabolism; nap when I can in a sunny spot on the floor and allow myself the indulgence of being a grass roller, often reveling in the lushness of summer lawns on my skin and the smell of new mown grass.

So on this particular afternoon, I happened into a particular pharmacy, which was on my route from home to the airport, but was one that I never had a reason to shop at before. I had realized suddenly that I had forgotten my supplements and stopped there to get enough to carry me over for a trip I was taking.

As usually happens whenever you're in a new pharmacy, you find all the products you want but none of the brands you're familiar with, so what would usually take thirty seconds to grab a couple of bottles off a shelf now takes thirty minutes as you have to hunt, read, compare and evaluate.

"No."

If there is a shorter statement in the human language which get's the same definitive response, I don't know what it would be. You're taught the basic rules of "no" as a baby: stop, drop, and/or eat whatever you're holding before Mom takes it away. In this case, I simply stopped.

"Excuse me?" I asked, hesitating with the current bottle in mid-pull between shelf and reading distance.

"No," she said again from behind me, "that's not what you want."

"How?"

I didn't say "the hell," but I thought it.

She looked me right in the eye, "Chromium and carnitine, you're a weight lifter, right?"

"No" was the answer on my lips, but when I turned to confront her I immediately discovered Wendy was hot, and I wasn't prepared for her looks or her smile, so what came out was a startled "Yeah."

I lied. Sometimes, as an older married guy, you need to live the fantasy when you can and I wasn't expecting the "no" to have come from a Pam Anderson look-a-like who paid me a vague semi-compliment by wrongly thinking I was a weight lifter. So, I lied. It's a male brain-stem testosterone thing that happens to almost all guys when they are over thirteen, so sue me (but don't tell my wife).

"Yeah I'm a weight lifter. (Liar!) But I'm just starting out. (Liar - liar - pants - on - fire!) Isn't this what I should take?"

"No," flat answer, "it's not what you should take."

Wait a second, I had read a lot, done some research and taken this stuff before with favorable results. Was I missing something? Wasn't I capable of guiding myself here?

Or could she be a Professional Guide?

As I was trying to get a quick read on her Guide skills I realized, from outward appearances, Wendy wouldn't be easy to pick out as a Guide. She lacked the classical accoutrements of someone who really means business, yet had the demeanor and confidence of a Professional Guide. She conversed with directness and straight-forwardness and her voice commanded attention.

But, Wendy also appeared not to be wearing a shirt under her pharmacy jacket, which was awful distracting to her dialog, since she's what my mother used to refer to as an *ample woman,* my wife refers to as *eye candy* and my son simply refers to as *nice*. Ergo, the problem was I could see by her outfit that she was a Pharmacist (Certified Specialist), and that she had the training to direct my selection of products that filled my needs, but I didn't know if she would prove to be a capable Professional Guide too, and thereby have the ability to offer beneficial advice. **Remember, this is the important distinction between an ordinary Certified Specialist and a Certified Specialist** *who is also* **a trained Professional Guide.** I wanted to find out which she was, so I fished.

"What do you think I should be taking?"

"Let me show you," and I obediently followed a great pair of legs in heels. She gave me her name, "I'm Wendy," and in an automated pre-programmed response I believe I gave her mine back.

```
In truth, I never fully heard her give her
name even though I had responded with mine. It
was later, at the end of the sale, when she
handed me her card that I actually caught her
```

name again and it stuck. I was too busy trying not to think about the legs I was thinking about the first time she said it.

On that note: Ladies, if you expect us to listen to every word, you'll need to watch what you wear. Don't stop wearing cute outfits, especially if you've got the shape to justify wearing them; just be aware that you'll need to repeat things often, depending on the cut of the blouse or the length of the skirt. Hooters Girls understand this. The most common answer for the simple question of "What can I get you?" is "I'm sorry, what did you say?"

Wendy, obviously used to men not paying complete attention to every word delivered, gently cleared her throat and smiled as I came up from what was probably an all-too-typical male daydream I must have slipped into involving her. As the dream faded, the realization that we had stopped walking several seconds ago became embarrassingly obvious, since my attention wasn't on the bottle she had been attempting to show me.

"This is better. It's simpler, balanced, more convenient and will save you money," Wendy said, getting me back to the real world.

She handed me a bottle of *Super-Hydro-Maxi-Lite©*, a concoction in pill form which had both ingredients plus "a whole lot more." I guess the phrase "a whole lot more" covers all the other ingredients and allows for the use of the adjectives *"super"* and *"maxi"* in the name. I could only assume that the *"hydro"* had something to do with water which seemed ironic since this was in pill form and not suspension, and the "lite" probably meant it had half the calories of *'Classic'-Super-Hydro-Maxi©* if such a product ever existed.

I rolled the bottle over and looked at the pill count on the bottle, then went to the price clearly stamped on the top sticker.

Fantasies put on hold for now, I began to question her abilities again. I wanted it not to be true, but this didn't look right. She doesn't even know her prices? A quick mental calculation had shown me right away that these would end up costing me significantly more than what I was currently taking. Price wasn't

The Retail Jungle

the issue, but a Professional Guide wouldn't make a blatant pricing mistake on a quote.

"I think you may be confused," my mouth moved while my mind kept telling my eyes not to talk to the cleavage. "These are more expensive." I handed the bottle over in a fashion that said "take a peek" while I tried desperately not to.

Wendy took the bottle, but already began her response before it was in her hand, "You would think so just from the price, but there's more to it than that."

A flat statement, and again that confidence. It opened the Professional Guide door to the beginning of a pharmacological Jungle tour, and I waltzed right on through without even looking back.

"There is?"

And she paused (and you know how much I love it when Guides take that pause before they do what they do), and she added a Farrah Faucett hair flip in slow motion, and I think there was the far-off sound of a few doves taking flight as a single ray of golden sun fell through some unseen window catching her in a heavenly spotlight (at least that's how I replay it in my mind), and she began.

"Yes. There is. Supplements are great, but too often it's easy to get overly impressed by the positive effects and overlook the negative effects. Chromium and carnitine like any supplement, like any drug, like anything you may put into your body," she touched my arm, creating gooseflesh, "comes with good points and bad. The key is balance, to maximize the good effects and minimize the bad."

"Ok." I was starting to be convinced Wendy was a definite Guide because of her sincerity. Sometimes you can pick up on a Professional Guide's skills and experience by the way they talk about the products or services they represent. Sometimes it takes more. I wanted more.

"What kind of side effects could I possibly get from a supplement? I mean, if it were really hazardous then it would only be sold with a prescription, wouldn't it?"

Wendy smiled, "You know, they sell drain cleaner on aisle sixteen. You can get that without a prescription too. Feel like drinking some?"

"Point well taken," I admitted. "But what could be the hazard with a mineral supplement?" I had never heard of any real issues.

She took another moment to pause reflectively, and then continued.

"Well, carnitine can impair thyroid hormone action, so you shouldn't take it if you have low thyroid hormone levels, but besides that it can produce a rapid heart rate, an increase in blood pressure, fever and headaches."

My jaw dropped, with that one fact she'd just taken control as **The Expert**.

Wendy chuckled, "You think that's bad? Some laboratory studies using cell cultures and animals have suggested chromium picolinate causes oxidative stress and DNA damage."

"WHAT!?!" I almost fainted.

"You bet," she said.

"There's no way," I shook my head.

Tourists, finding themselves lost, often get overcome by immediate disbelief and disorientation. It's the same feeling experienced hikers get when they realize that, in spite of all their planning they are lost in the woods, and it's scary.

Several years ago, I was watching *The Clair Witch Project* on DVD. I had never seen the movie in theatres but heard how scary it was supposed to be, with supernatural events and a film crew getting attacked. I was so terrified by that movie I practically threw up. It had nothing to do with the witch, the murders or anything supernatural. It was the scene where the crew tried to hike back out of the site for four hours only to realize they were totally lost in the woods.

I've been there. That's happened to me.

Seeing it portrayed caused my stomach to flip and shake so violently that my dinner was almost ejected. Later, at the movie's climactic ending where the kids are being tormented by the spirits and are running around the abandoned house screaming, I was almost gleefully relieved. "Oh, thank God! At least they're not lost in the woods anymore!"

I was almost that scared now. Wendy saw my fright and came to the rescue.

"Jeff," she smiled, "It's OK. You would need to take a bunch, probably way more then you've ever taken, but why tempt fate? Look, this company has done tons of research." She handed me back the bottle, "Besides a balanced clinically tested amount of chromium and carnitine, this company adds several known antioxidants to the mix for increased protection against cellular damage. They also added B, C and E vitamins, all of which have positive effects on blood pressure."

"But, the price. You said it would save me money. How can that be?"

Wendy started taking bottle after bottle from the shelf to make her point. "If you bought everything separately," bottle after bottle she stacked up, "this is what you'd be buying."

I looked at all the price stickers facing me and admitted she was obviously right.

"Also, the dosage balance would require that you take some half and quarter tablets to equal everything out. Isn't convenience worth something?"

She was right again.

I helped her replace all the individual bottles and once again picked up and handed her the one bottle of `Super-Hydro-Maxi-Lite` ™.

"Ring it up," I said.

Wendy took two more bottles, identical to mine, from the shelf.

"There's a special. Buy two and the third is free." She smiled. "I told you I was going to save you money."

Lesson #13 - Guides build each sale. A Professional Guide knows how to maximize discounts, package pricing, rebates, incentives and purchasing multiples to achieve the maximum benefit for Tourists.

CHAPTER ELEVEN
The 100% Experience

No matter how you feel about sales, a job **IS** a job, and being an Encyclopedia Salesman was my job at the time, so I was expected to do it, both by myself and my company.

I know a statement about being "expected to do it" shocks some people, especially those who hold tremendous disdain for the rigors of daily working. You know the type, people who are hired to do something, anything, but would rather spend the day complaining about their tasks than doing their tasks. They are in every profession and it doesn't even matter how exalted or lowly the position or pay, they just don't really want to work.

I can never understand how they get hired, but they are in almost every company in the world.

I've never been one of those. Oh, don't get me wrong; I've found myself in many a situation where I couldn't see myself doing the task at hand, but I've always either quit, or had the blessing of being let go when I informed superiors of my refusal.

Quitting is good for you sometimes. It's you voicing your opinion, "No. I believe you're mistaken. I wasn't hired to perform that particular task and I'm not going to do that." Being honest with yourself and your superiors is a good thing to do from time to time, especially when you have the turpitude to back up your claim by walking away should they insist.

Being fired is good too, because it's your employer having the strength to say, "You can't perform as we expected, and we need someone else who can perform these tasks without hesitancy."

That's honest, and more companies should let people go who won't do the job at hand.

But the world has become a legal and human resources garden, weeded with "those who won't" and often managed by "those who can't," making it harder on "us who honestly want to, if given the opportunity."

I call this the "Pro-Migrant-Worker Philosophy of Employment" and many people I know support it. We are the group that loves it when someone says, "Migrant workers are taking all the jobs!" so we can ask, "Do you want to go pick tomatoes all day for five dollars an hour?" They took a job offered and want to do it, and do their best. When the offending person states that they wouldn't do the job since they are much more skilled, we continue, "Then what the hell are you complaining about?"

Although, in my heart of hearts, I know there must also be a migrant worker somewhere complaining daily as he toils, "I hate this stinking job" yet still picking just enough tomatoes to barely keep his position - and his foreman is just complacent enough to let him keep picking while thinking, "I wish this guy would quit so I could hire that rich white college kid who applied. He looked like a tomato pickin' pendejo!"

An advantage to most jobs is the **training phase**. This is the period where you are expected to move from **liability** to **asset** for a company, and absorb the skills along the way to make you **productive**.

Every company has a phase-in similar to this, whether formalized or not, and it's usually worthless, simply because the measure of an employee becomes apparent when a situation turns from the expected to the unexpected, and nobody ever gets trained for the unexpected.

For instance, let's look at *McDingle's*™, probably the best known hamburger place in the world, and home of the *"Whipper©,"* a monster burger that *"...takes three hands to eat*™*"* and is fronted by *"Jerk*™*,"* their spokesman, that guy on the TV ads with the big square head.

Working at McDingle's is the first job many people get. They have a rigorous ninety-day employee orientation program in which they teach everything about making every product they sell from the Whipper right down to their fries. Matter of fact, they spend five days alone on the FRY-MASTER 8200©-the Grand Pooh-Bah of deep fryers. They teach you everything you could possibly run into on a daily, weekly and monthly basis with the FM8200.

Now, on day ninety-one, the new hire is ready to fly solo and is put in charge of the FM8200. He, (or **she** - I'm not sexist or picky; as long as the drive-up line gets moving and there's no additional hair or tentacle pieces in my "Breakfast Whipper with cheese, egg and fried pickles," it can be a six-legged alien doing the cooking for all I care) starts up the fryer and there's an electrical "pop!" followed by the smell of burning lard as the FM8200 has a melt-down and is now engulfed in flames.

By the way, this is a 1 in 500,000 chance electrical flaw which is ever so slightly possible in the FM8200, and which, I understand, *FryCo Industries*™ has totally eliminated in the new FM8201-b$^{(pat.\ pending)}$.

So here is the true test of an employee, after all the extensive effort that went into interviewing the right person from the thousands of applicants:

Are you a member of PETA?
No.
You're hired! You start today!

When the fryer pops into flame, all ninety days of training are out the window, because the longevity of the building itself is staked on the innate smarts of a kid and his decision on which of the two available options to throw on the inferno - a sixty-four ounce FountainBrew© or a metal vat cover.

Luckily, there is another phase to training which is invaluable. It's referred to differently for different occupations, but the one I like best comes from the waitresses. It's known as **shadowing**, and, put simply, it's when a new waitress just follows along with a skilled waitress and does nothing but watch to understand the flow of ordering. This tag-along goes on for several days and is great, because on a daily basis the new employee probably sees several out-of-the-ordinary situations handled, and gets a feel for how to tackle the unexpected.

Luckily, McDingle's has a similar training phase in that ninety days, so Renaldo, the last Fry-Jockey can inform Jennifer the new Fry-Jockette, about last Tuesday.

"Jenn, you should have seen it! Whole 8200 blazing! Smoke alarms are clanging, little kids are screaming. But guess what? Luckily, I had seen that kid's special on *PBS*, like last week, and knew you should never-ever throw a liquid like a *FountainBrew©* on a grease fire because that little "C" in the circle right after the name stands for "**C**an't throw this stuff on grease fires" (most people don't know that), so if that ever happens again you need to throw that metal vat-cover on the thing, because there's no little "C" in *vat-cover*. Wait. I mean, there *IS* a little "C" in vat-cover, but it's not *circled*, so I think it's like totally OK."

Forgive Renaldo's naiveté. As we all know, the little circled "C" actually stands for "copyright" and has nothing to do with the possible flame aggravating properties of FountainBrew©. The reason the vat-cover is the proper choice is because a metal vat-cover will suffocate the flames. You should never throw any liquids on a grease fire, but a lid or a metal cover will do in a pinch if you don't have an approved chemical fire extinguisher immediately available. And, you should never throw flour, especially specific brands of flour which have their names followed by the little "C" in a circle.

I received waitress-type shadow training for selling encyclopedias from my supervisor and direct Territory Sales Manager, and this guy was a piece of work. He had to be. I learned immediately that there is no **standard sale** when it involves being in a person's home. Not that I didn't get some standardized training; I did. But I realized on day one that I might as well throw most of it out the window if I was going to survive.

The Territory Manager I had the good fortune to travel with was named Phil, and he was a visual phenomenon. Fifty-ish, with thin collar-length hair, greasy and full of dandruff, a plaid sportcoat which had used up its better days of wear, a too-wide tie with various unknown stains from past meals and white socks.

I liked the man at first sight. You had to. If today you typed "worn out sales icon" into a web browser looking for images, his would be exactly what you'd expect to pull up. It's hard not to like something, even something bad, that is such an exact representation of what we expect.

So, as part of my orientation, I traveled my first week, which was three evenings from six to nine, and made calls shadowing Phil.

You would think Phil would have been a slippery, snake-oil type of guy, but he wasn't. He knew every classical close in the book and used them with reckless abandon, but when the customer gave a final 'no,' he respected it.

I owe the discovery of one of my favorite sales lessons to Phil.

It was on the drive to the last call on the second day when Phil swore to close the next sale. We had been having what he called a "tough week," since Phil historically closed one of every two calls he made. He blamed his failures this week on me, pointing out that the only variation to his normal calls was my presence. Still, in a one-hundred-percent commission world, a paycheck depended on a sale and Phil was determined to end tonight on a financially positive note.

According to the manual, `(yeah - they gave us a manual)`, you could tell a lot about a person's willingness to be sold by how their home was appointed. I guess the thought was people who spent money improving their surroundings probably spent money improving their minds. Phil said that was crap, but he did say, "Bookshelves mean books. If you see bookshelves in the living room, you got a better than fifty-percent chance that they will buy because people who put those in the living room are trying to impress visitors with how smart they are. Nothing says smart like a set of encyclopedias sitting on a bookshelf in plain view."

`(Good tip, but that's not the one I was referring to.)`

The people were home, a good sign as I came to realize, since seventy-five percent of my future "appointments" were never there at the pre-scheduled time. And, they were actually willing to listen, another good sign, since the remaining quarter of my future appointments, who actually happened to be in residence when they said they would, usually met me through the open crack of a chained door with a surprised look and a barked message of, "What the freak do you want?!?"

Phil did his sales spiel, and the people watched and listened obligingly, paying enough attention to avoid being rude. I was sitting off to the side watching Phil do his thing, and kind of keeping an eye on the couple's children so the parents could focus on what Phil had to say.

Phil pulled out some pamphlets, which supported many of the points he was making about the scholastic achievements of children from homes where encyclopedias were made available - a valid discussion point which moments earlier he had shared with the family. They read them, passed them back and forth and then stared politely, again waiting. He tried several closes, but when it came to the end of the presentation and the decision was on the line, the answer was evident.

"You know," the H.O.T.H. (Head of the household) said, "they look great, but we're just not interested. Besides, our kids are still pretty young, and they would tear those books to pieces before they were old enough to get much use out of them."

Phil jumped in, picking up on the issue of quality, "Are you kidding, look how strongly these are bound!" and he picked up the entire volume by one page, a demo trick we were taught in orientation.

"No really," said H.O.T.H., "we're not interested."

You could tell that Phil was bitter. He had wanted to impress me with both a sale and his closing prowess, but these people obviously had issues that, coupled with the lack of visible bookshelvery, added up to a big zero on his sales register.

As he began to pack up his presentation materials, he was oblivious to the fact that I was over on the side, kind of playing with the couple's kids who must have been all of five and three.

Suddenly, the S.O.T.H. (Spouse of the House) screamed, "Winston! NO!"

Winston (can you believe they named a baby Winston? Winston and Virginia - I guess they were smokers) had the volume I handed him by a single page and was spinning around with the book fluttering in the cyclonic breeze. Virginia was clapping her hands and laughing; I was just watching and smiling.

"If he rips that you're going to have to buy it!" exclaimed Phil with way too much enthusiasm. You could almost hear the "Rip! Rip! Rip!" chant going on in his head.

As S.O.T.H. and H.O.T.H. made a dash, I simply reached over and put a hand on Winston's shoulder, stopping the flight path, and took the volume while he sat down with a thump, dizzy from the experience.

"Look," I said to the parents fanning the pages, "no harm, no foul. You don't ever have to worry about these pages coming out, they really are bound exceptionally. The pages are heavy bond with a gloss finish and a high tensile strength, durable and easy to clean. These are meant to be used and enjoyed by the entire family for a long, long time."

We left with the order for a complete set, which Phil slammed down on the corporate office sales desk the second we returned to headquarters, in a flash of triumph to both his credit, and his paycheck's. I got nothing from that sale, monetarily.

What I did get was a sales strategy that has stuck in my mind and has served me well as a Professional Guide. I had also learned how to correctly use advertising, in the form of pamphlets, ads or brochures, as a sales tool instead of as a marketing tool.

Lesson #14 – There are three types of Guide recommendations in this world: a one percent, a ten percent, and a hundred percent. A one-percent recommendation is a spoken recommendation. A written recommendation is ten times stronger in the eyes of the Tourist simply because it's in print. (Hand a Tourist advertising that confirms a point you're making as a Guide and it becomes an instant sales tool.) ***But a hundred-percent recommendation is a tactile recommendation, something the Tourist can see, feel, smell, touch or taste. It turns the imaginary into the practical, and the possible into the probable.*** **Tourists like the experience.**

To ever really be successful as a Professional Guide, you have to have faith in the fact that Tourists like the experience. It explains a lot about how sales should be handled. Tourists want the experience; they enjoy the experience; they expect the experience - and you need to give it to them.

Look around at how sales are handled, and by accepting the basic truth, (that Tourists don't just want to **purchase**, but that they want an **experience**), you will understand how many seemingly irrational sales techniques came into existence.

Here's an example:

Why do they make everybody "test drive" a car before buying it?

To prove the car can be driven? All cars can be driven.

The reason for a test drive goes deeper than "experiencing the driving phenomenon that *Car&Chauffer Magazine*© calls; 'The thrill of moving while sitting still.'" It's the experience.

```
By the way, please remember, the little "C"
in a circle after the magazine name means you
should probably never throw this particular
magazine on a grease fire, even one in a car.
```

While it's obvious that you're buying a car for transportation, you don't need to experience transportation. Transportation isn't an experience; it's a concept. And once you've grasped a concept - enter here, drive there, exit there, and repeat as necessary - that's pretty much all anyone needs to do. You drove to the dealership; we must assume you pretty much get the concept of cars and driving.

Test-drives, however, are not about driving or transportation. They are about all the sensual things which are either new if you're a first-time buyer, or have been long forgotten if you've owned your previous car more than a few months.

The shine of the unblemished highly waxed paint; the solid clunk of the car door as it shuts on brand new rubber seals; the smell of leather that hasn't been smeared with dirt, grease, dust, food, vomit, baby poop or an occasionally spilled *MoonDoe's Coff-a-chino*©. The windows aren't covered with handprints or nose-prints, and the air vents don't rattle from someone who wondered, as six-year-olds often do, if those little mint candies will not only fit through the grates, but will provide entertainment when, and if, they came flying out again once the fan is turned on.

Nothing stinks, sticks or squeaks. Nothing rattles, requires battles or smells like cattle's. Everything works and is luxuriant to the touch, clean, crisp and new.

Of course, it's a new car! What else could you possibly expect? But the wonderful thing is, as Tourists, even though we've been there before, we do forget, and we are all ready to experience everything again and again.

Think of this as it applies to trips and vacations. It could explain why we are drawn back to locations, year upon year, which we have already experienced and visited. We want that experience rush again; in our hearts we crave it, and as much as we remember our vacation to Cancun and what a great time it was last winter, we forget that the water actually is that amazing blue until we see it again with our own eyes.

We are a tactile group of Tourists. We love the experience and we love to sell ourselves, so we want a little taste of what's coming.

Whole strategies for sales in retail Jungles hinge around this point:

- Taste the Gooddiva™ chocolate. Maybe you want to buy a pound for Valentine's Day?
- Feel the bed linens on the sample bed at Sleep, Soak & Sometime™. Wouldn't you sleep comfortably on these?
- Just a spritz of perfume on this little piece of cardboard as you walk through Dullards™. Now imagine how that scent will drive your husband wild on your anniversary.
- Listen to this stereo at Circuit Buy™. Can you hear the difference Dulbe™ Noise Retraction makes to an opera?
- Look at this BrownRay™ and HDTV, as compared to this old DVD player and television combination. Wouldn't you like to see every player's nose hairs during the next televised cricket match?

But when I was selling encyclopedias, it wasn't until a few weeks later that I understood how tactile Tourist's interests could become during a tour.

Phil had imparted his wisdom upon me, or so the Sales Director believed, since our shadowing week had ended with four sales. The one previously mentioned, and all three on our last day where Phil allowed me to "show what I had learned" by handling each sale from the knock at the door up to filling out the sales order. Of course, when it came to filling out the sales order and writing in the name of the person who should receive commission for the sale, then Phil, as a help to me since I was still technically a trainee, would obligingly jump in and complete all the "complicated fine print" as he liked to call it.

The Sales Director complimented Phil on that Friday when he submitted my three orders as his own.

"Wow, buddy, you never fail to amaze me!," and then to me, "I hope you paid attention, you got to learn from a Master."

Had I had made a stink I guess I could have got Phil to split some of the commission with me. After all, I was really the one who figured out the one percent, ten percent, hundred percent routine. But Phil grows on you - people like that often do - and I was happy for him. Besides, next week I was on my own and I would get every penny of whatever I earned. It didn't appear that the job was going to be that tough. Thinking over the past week I began to dream of what I would do with the money I was going to make.

CHAPTER TWELVE
Someone Will Buy

Nightmare.

It's been four weeks of visiting homes that have all the charm of a dumpster, yet none of the pleasant smells or uplifting indirect lighting. My dreams of easy money had evaporated, leaving only the chilly reality that I was going to get nothing close to the situation that I had experienced during my time as a trainee.

Had I had any idea of the caliber of leads I was going to be assigned, the area of the city or the danger, I might never have taken on the effort, but I had not and so I did my best.

It was summer, and one of those really hot Midwestern nights that I remember from when I was a kid and we had no air conditioning - when you just know you're not going to get any decent sleep because it's too hot, too humid, and you're torn between the feeble relief offered by the slight breeze of an electric fan and annoyance at the constant tic-tic-tic of its motor.

I don't know what possessed me to make this last call, since I wouldn't be arriving until almost nine-thirty at night and that broke one of the few rules defined as company etiquette.

```
From page 17 of the handbook: "Do not begin
calls later than 9:00 pm as a courtesy to the
client… who may claim "sleep deprivation" as an
alibi when they discover that the quick "30
minute presentation" usually runs ninety minutes
as you try to work about a dozen closes on the
H.O.T.H., S.O.T.H., C.O.T.H., and of course when
```

necessary the P.O.T.H. if you become desperate enough."

But one of our Call Center Operators happened to find a "potential" (that's a name given by Operators to Clients who agreed to see a Rep) home by the phone at 9:15 pm, congratulated them on winning one of the "grand prizes," and when she tried to schedule an appointment found that the clients worked odd hours, and now was the only time we were likely to catch them both at home - at least that's what she told me as a justification to break etiquette and head over to their home.

Still, I wouldn't normally have done this, preferring to be out of this area of town before total darkness took hold, but our Call Center Operators got twenty bucks for every lead they turned into a potential. And this particular Call Center Operator was just into her twenties, was really good looking and had a reputation for being liberal with her affections for Sales Reps, especially new Sales Reps who gave her potentials priority. I was new, and I've always been curious about reputations, especially those involving twenty-year-olds and their liberties, so obviously I agreed. I also agreed to share a bottle of wine Saturday night with the operator so she could thank me in person.

The address must have been a mistake, since the numbers on the buildings didn't seem to follow any sequential order in this part of town. I had driven past the only apartment-type dwelling anywhere close to where I guessed the address had to be situated at least four times before I concluded that this must be the location, missing numbers or not.

It didn't help that the street light appeared to have been shot out in some crazy attempt to make this already morbidly dark slum vanish into complete blackness.

Two bushes had grown up next to the building's entrance but had never seen the handiwork of a set of shears and now loomed monstrously in the darkness, their spindly wild branches reaching up over a dozen feet and strewn with debris, paper shreds and broken Styrofoam cups that had been snatched from the wind. They appeared to be growing from mounds of cans and broken beer bottles, which hid any dirt or rock in which they were originally planted.

The facade was old grey brick, covered with the soot of traffic, neglect and despair. The door was set back in a recessed alcove without the benefit of any welcoming overhead illumination. This added to the impression that I was entering something more akin to a gigantic maw than a building entrance.

A lighter supplied enough visibility to read the names on the roster. Next to 4C I found the potential's name, "Waters." I buzzed, waited, buzzed again, wanted to leave, crossed my fingers that the last buzz would go like the previous two and buzzed again.

"Yeah?" it could have been "Hey," "Yes" or even "Get bent" for all I could make out, the intercom having seen better days. I assumed it was "Yeah?"

"Ms. Waters? Hi, I'm Jeff. I'm here from the encyclopedia company. I was told this would be a good time for us to drop off your award certificate and do a brief presentation on our educational materials. Is this a good time?"

There was some quick response which was cut off by a buzz signaling an invitation.

"It had better be more than a reputation," I remember thinking about this call and why I was making it now.

Describing the building sounds too stereotypical, so I'll just use the phrase, "It was in disrepair." The walls, the stairs, the roaches, the trash, even the graffiti was in disrepair.

This really says a lot, since I have found that though you can say a lot about problems associated with folks who practice the ritual of graffiti, one thing you can't say is, "they're lazy." I've had graffiti on a building removed at six in the evening only to find it right back there in complete color at four the next morning. Honestly, I can't get paid employees to show up before eight, but these graffiti people are dedicated. Add to that, they bring their own tools, never take a lunch break and, I'm gathering from some of the odd places I've seen graffiti like high bridge overpasses, water towers and cliffs, they appear to have some sort of acrobatic training as a standard skill set. All of this, with an eye for style, color,

```
format,   perspective   and   creativity   makes
"Taggers" a huge untapped labor resource. I can't
be   the   only   person   to   notice   this.   Trust   me,
somewhere in a tomato field there is a foreman
thinking, "I wish these lazy guys would quit so I
could hire those Taggers who keep marking up my
tool shed. Those cabrones would make some tomato
pickin' pendejos!"
```

I located 4C, knocked, and was forced to bite the inside of my cheek. The woman who answered the door appeared to be all of twenty five, black in that exotic sexy 80s way most women don't even try to emulate. Her make-up was stating the she was going out for the evening, but her clothing said she was in for the night. An almost see-through crepe baby doll top and a tiny matching satin bikini bottom were all that she deemed appropriate to cover a voluptuous physique. I couldn't blame her; the apartment was still almost ninety degrees, though the sun had already set.

(Don't stare, don't stare, don't stare!) "Mrs. Waters?"

"Yeah," she smiled with perfect white teeth, "did you bring me my prize?"

(Oh, sweet merciful God, keep eye contact.) "Yes Ma'am. I've got your prize envelope with me. As part of our promotion, I'm supposed to give you a quick informational presentation on our encyclopedias, so if you're one of our grand prize winners, you're able to enjoy all the features included and take full advantage of your new set and our services. Is Mr. Waters home?" I asked as I looked around.

She had escorted me into a modestly appointed living room that appeared quite nice and was way out of place for this building, neighborhood and district. She indicated a cream leather sofa where I seated myself in such a way as to present to both H.O.T.H. and S.O.T.H.

```
From page 6 of the handbook; "ALWAYS present
while  facing  the  clients,  and  positioned  in  such
a  way  that  you  can  maintain  full  visual  contact
with all Potentials. By presenting in this manner
you   avoid   the   Spouse   behind   you   mouthing   the
```

```
words 'No Way' and making the 'slash across the
throat motion,' which we have found can be
detrimental to your closing."
```

She spoke softly, "Joe, um, Mr. Waters is taking a nap right now; he works very early." She sat down next to me on the sofa, uncomfortably close, her thigh touching mine. "I was hoping you could just show me your little presentation," her hand fell on my knee.

`(Oh dear Lord, her top was falling open, not that the material hid much to begin with.)` "Mrs. Waters, maybe this isn't the best time," I said with my voice cracking - something I couldn't recall it doing since I was thirteen.

"Sugar, it's now or never. Let me hear what you got."

`(What the heck!)` "Ok," pulling a volume from my bag, "Let me show you the world at your finger tips," and into the presentation I went.

I've heard that professionals everywhere experience this same phenomenon. For some reason, when you immerse yourself in doing what you're trained to do, routine takes over. My mother was like that. She had worked as a secretary for many years and my brother and I were always amazed when we called her at work, at how charming and benevolent her voice sounded, "Structural Products Incorporated, Rose speaking. How may I help you?" It was nothing like the sometimes harsh sounds we were used to hearing.

"If you two don't stop fighting and finish your mashed potatoes `(rutabaga, yuck!)`, I'm going to tan your tails with my slipper!"

Weird, she could be yelling at us like that and the phone would ring, and mid swing with the slipper she could answer and we would hear the *phone voice* saying, "Marjorie, would you please hold for a moment?" just as sweetly as if she was interrupted during afternoon tea.

My *phone voice* was my presentation. Once I said those words, "Let me show you the world" I became the Encyclopedia Guide. All thought about Mrs. Waters, what she was or wasn't wearing, the building, the neighborhood, vanished. It was just me, doing what I was meant to do - guiding a Tourist.

Mr. Waters woke up about an hour later when he heard me and Mrs. Waters (Genevieve, isn't that a pretty first name?) laughing over some of the more interesting pictures of orangutans. He seemed oblivious to the fact that his wife was dressed as she was, undoubtedly a supporter of the "if you got it, flaunt it" mentality.

When I finished my presentation, they both gave a hard final look at the set, the terms and everything I had put forth on the table. They signed the form which stated, "We have received a full presentation and accept our gift within the terms and conditions of the prize rules, blah, blah, blah…"

Mr. Waters actually loved the steak knives, because, I believe, he was one of those gracious people who never look a gift horse in the mouth, even if its mouth is full of cheap steak knives.

That would probably be the end of the story, except for what happened that following Saturday night.

I did get that date with the Call Center Operator; although I must admit that, as unfair as it seems, from that day forward I have tended to rate *all* women physically against Mrs. Waters, and the Operator, having been recently re-rated in such close temporal proximity to my initial encounter with that incredible icon of femininity, had dropped significantly on my *Hubba-Hubba Scale*.

Yet there we were, enjoying a bottle of *Spoon's Ranch Pink Catawba Wine©* and trying to see whose tongue could reach the other's tonsils first, when she informed me that she was going to get up and change into something more comfortable for the heat. Mentally, I crossed my fingers and chanted, "Crepe baby doll, crepe baby doll," all the while wondering - if I turned down the lights a little, would she appear tanner?

"Thanks for making that call the other night," she shouted from the bedroom, "I really needed that extra twenty this month."

Realizing that I had picked up my paycheck as well but hadn't even bothered to open it, I pulled the folded envelope from my pocket. I don't know why I bothered to look just then, since I knew it was going to be eighty five dollars; the "draw" that was paid weekly if you failed to make any sales. This week had been a complete bust, which happens sometimes, even to Professional Guides like me.

Unfolding the flap, I pulled the check up so the numbers just crested the edge. "That can't be right," I thought, and pulled it out a little further.

The words matched the numbers, so the chance of a typo was limited, although I was still in shock. One thousand four hundred and thirty dollars. I pulled the entire check from the envelope and opened it up to reveal the payout structure listed on the stub. There it stated the name of the clients who actually purchased that week. Three times the name *Waters* appeared.

The set ran eight hundred and seventy-one dollars; our commission was four hundred dollars a set. We also received an extra one hundred dollars for each set that was sold from a referral. Listed by the names was four hundred, then five hundred, and again another five hundred. That came to fourteen hundred dollars, minus two weeks "draw" at eighty five dollars each, leaving the fourteen-thirty.

"Holy hand-grenades!"

I called Joe and Genevieve the next week under the premise of following-up, to be certain they had received their sets in good order, but what I really wanted to know was what on earth happened.

Joe answered the phone, sounding sleepy on the fifth ring, "Yeah?"

"Mr. Waters," I began, "its Jeff from the Encyclopedia Company."

We talked and everything was great; the sets had been delivered and there were no issues.It seems Joe was the head of maintenance for a local high school. After my presentation he went back to work and started poking around the high school library reference section.

I had shown him where to find the printing and copyright dates in the front of each addition and he had wanted to know if the volumes at the high school where he worked were current. As it turns out, they were almost twenty years old. Now that doesn't sound like a lot, but remember all the changes that happened in the 60s and 70s? None of that was included in the school's antiquated set.

Joe made his case to the school Principal for an updated set for the high school library. The Principal agreed, and that was referral number one.

The Principal at the high school was close with the Principal at the junior high, who checked the volumes there - same dates - and this became referral number two.

I was still in doubt about the original set, so I asked and got the answer.

"Well, we weren't saying anything right away; you know how superstitious families are about this, but Gennie is pregnant. She just found out about it two weeks ago.

We've been living in this apartment, slowly buying furniture because we are saving for a house. We closed on it Monday, a few days before we met with you. So, we are moving to a new home, expecting a new baby and basically starting a whole new portion of our lives.

After you came by, Gennie and I talked about our baby and the future. You really made us think about what we want for our children. It didn't take long; we knew right away. We want our baby to have everything we can give. We want it to **have the world**."

I sent them a card the next week with the following note and a crisp one-hundred dollar bill:

```
"J&G, I hope the baby has every opportunity
in the world. Read to him or her every night from
a different volume. The words don't matter when
they are young; it's just the sound of your voice
and spending time with your baby. May your god
watch over you all - Jeff"
```

Lesson #15 – Someone will buy. There are times when being a Guide places stress on you: financial stress, emotional stress, and occupational stress. You will always have times of plenty and times where sales seem very difficult. In those difficult times remember: it's all a numbers game. Present to everybody, eventually you will be rewarded with sales. Someone is always out there ready to take your Tour and make the purchase; you just need to find them.

CHAPTER THIRTEEN
To Guide or Not to Guide

Computers held a certain romantic attraction for those of us who came of age during the 70's, but I don't believe it was the inception of the personal computer that caused the interest to peak. I attribute every advancement in electronics directly to video games.

Video games are addictive, not in a general television-watching sort of way, but in a more concentrated direct-to-the-brain format that stimulates as it obliterates. Video games are to television what I imagine `crack` is to `cocaine`, and like `crack`, it's exponentially more addictive.

I've heard a philosophy used often when drugs are discussed, particularly marijuana. It's said, "Pot is not awfully bad in and of itself `(when compared to the detrimental effects of smoking tobacco or drinking alcohol)`, but pot is a *gateway* drug, often leading to more dangerously potent drugs in an attempt to regain that first time high feeling."

For anyone familiar with video games - was there every a more true statement than this about the advancements made in video gaming systems?

I remember the first time I played *Ping*©. I think I dropped eighty dollars in quarters into that machine just bouncing a little dot from side to side. But Ping was a gateway game, just like every video game since.

Growing up, my family played a lot of board games, but I can't remember a time when I would have spent seven hours straight playing, or even wanting to play, a board game.

Over the years I have moved from video game to video game, buying system after system and game after game trying to recapture that initial high.

If you think it's just me, look around. I see grown adults paying big money to carry some new *Greenberry*™ device, preaching that they need the technology to remain constantly in touch with business contacts, only to allow a call to go to voicemail because they are involved in a game of *'Super Spumoni Brothers 8©.'*

Home computers have evolved to be faster and faster, with better graphics and sound, with larger memories - for what? A spread sheet? A word processor? Do you know how fast you'd have to be able to type to out-type even a 1970s computer? You can't do it. So what drove chip manufacturers to push the envelope again and again if not games and their associated graphics?

And if you're wondering why there was, and still is, a boom in home computers, its simple - nobody wants to spend seven hours in a library playing video games. Once the Internet exploded everybody had to have a computer in their home.

Personally, I hated to see it come, this boom in home computers. But I immediately realized it was going to make a huge impact on encyclopedia purchases.

Professional Guides are intuitive; we are very aware of trends and can almost be precognitive when it comes to purchasing opinions. A slowing of sales fervor coupled with some comments from potentials about *"holding off on the purchase for now"* and "I would buy, but I just bought" sets off the mental alarms and we start examining our situation. In this way, businesses can use Professional Guides as an indicator (like rats leaving a sinking ship), to keep an eye on the market trends. It was like that in encyclopedias, a gentle shift of the wind and I knew, along with several others, that the encyclopedia gravy-train had left the station.

Since I had gone directly from high school into the work force, I had skipped college. Now seemed to be a great chance to retrace my steps, take some time and refill my skills basket before setting off on my next employment path.

I took the entry tests and was immediately accepted at the college of my choice for the upcoming semester. Since computers had taken my job, I figured the best way to get even was go into electronic engineering, computer sciences, graphic design and Spanish.

> The Spanish was an afterthought. I was living in Southern California and met an incredibly beautiful - *a solid nine on the new Mrs.-Waters-Adjusted Hubba-Hubba Scale* - Columbian girl with the most amazing accent. On the weekends we would hop over the border to Tijuana, have a great dinner and spend the evening watching jai alai in the arena on Avenida de Revolución. Since she was so eye-catching, every guy we passed would make some comment, or wolf whistle or whisper something to the guy next to him, usually in Spanish. She spoke Spanish, naturally, and I didn't, so she would have to tell me what they said and we would laugh. One time, she refused to tell me what one hombre said, but I got the impression it wasn't nice or even cheeky or flirtatious. It was something down-right nasty. That was the weekend before I registered for classes. When I saw Spanish as an elective, there was no choice; I knew I had to learn Spanish if I was going to continue dating Latin women. I never became that fluent, but I can carry on a conversation and in the area of cursing; "Yo no soy un marinero, pero maldigo como uno!"

After two years the money got tight. I had made an appointment with the financial aid department, so I stopped in. I had already received a small scholarship due to my test scores, received a Pell Grant due to my current income level and had enough squirreled away to handle most of the remaining tuition. But after personally reviewing the situation, I quickly realized that it might be beneficial to have some extra funds coming in for little extras - like food, someplace to live and everything else not directly related to school during my last few months of classes.

"Damn," I thought, "I better get a job." (Brilliant is the college mind.)

It says in the Bible, "and the Lord God sayeth unto Job, 'Hey Dude, did you know I can see your house from up here?'" Just kidding. He sayeth, "Job, why doeth thou goest against the pricks?" This has always been one of my favorite verses because it's God saying, "Why are you trying to be something you're not?"

Some of us are Guides, some of us are not.

If you're good at painting, be an artist, or at least live your life doing things artistically. Work in graphic design, or be an architect. Do something that utilizes the gifts that your God provided you.

If you're a Guide, guide people. You know you will be happiest in life when you use the talents you have been given.

I am not good at painting. I am not an artist, an architect, a doctor or a plumber. I can try to learn these skills but I will never be as good at them as someone who has natural talent.

I guess I was attempting to "go against my pricks" by trying to become an engineer, and my God decided to give me a little push back toward the right track.

"Maybe you could get a part time job in sales to help you financially," suggested the Financial Aid Counselor at my college, "I've heard that **sales is simple**."

(You've got to be kidding me. Did she really just say that?)

With just a few credits remaining to complete my degree, instead of toughing it out and finishing my education while working part-time, I decided to look for a full-time job, concentrate on finances and put my studies on hold. My plan was to return in three months and finish. I never returned. I grew lazy. I can admit that. Once I began working, the desire to finish the degree faded. A steady paycheck, even from a boring job maintained my needs, and provided me a mental blanket to use as a cover for my head, so as to ignore the alarm clock of academic achievement. Every time that urge to return arose, I just hit the snooze button. Days passed. Days turned into weeks and then months as I became an automaton - waking, eating, working, then sleeping in a mindless cycle. I never returned.

Amongst other jobs, I'd dabbled in the optical industry. My brother was an optician for some time before he stopped going against his pricks, and eventually followed his artistic side into photography. Later he returned to the optical industry, blending his skills to become one of the best intra-ocular photographers around. It was a classic story of maximizing his natural talents into a career that allowed his artistic side to flourish, while providing stable income. I had assisted him on and off with lab work, which involves the fabrication of eyeglasses. Of course I didn't know what it was he was asking me to do originally.

"Would you like to come to work with me Saturday? We need some help at the clinic and you could use the money."

"Great!" because I did need the money. But I didn't know exactly what my brother did at the clinic, "What am I supposed to do?"

"You come with me and work as an optician."

"Alright! I've always found pregnant women kind of attractive. This should be…"

"Not obstetrician, dork, **optician**. We make eyeglasses." He seemed to regret having even suggested the idea.

"We make eyeglasses for pregnant women?" I knew now what he meant, but it was fun to get him riled up.

"Just be at my house Saturday morning; you can ride in with me."

We lived about half a mile away from each other, so this worked out fine. Saturday arrived and I showered, dressed and made my way over to by brother's after stopping by McDingle's for a Breakfast Whipper with cheese, egg and fried pickles to go.

He hadn't mentioned a dress code, so I had gone with the universal uniform of the unimaginative - black chino pants, a white oxford shirt and black shoes. This outfit was serviceable enough if the job involved labor, yet presentable enough if I was put in front of the public. Without more information on what opticians do on a daily basis, this would have to suffice for day one.

I realized Friday night that an exact time for morning departure hadn't been mentioned. I tried to call him all Friday evening, but my brother was one of those people we affectionately refer to as a "party animal" and his proclivity to be spending a Friday evening home by the phone was about nil. I had weighed the words clinic, morning and work, and followed my gut instinct to be ready and waiting on his front porch at six-thirty. I brought my breakfast and a magazine as well, so if he didn't leave until seven-thirty, I would be fed and entertained while I waited outside.

I've told this story dozens of times, and someone always asks quite surprised, "Why would you wait on the front porch at your own brother's house? Why wouldn't you just let yourself inside?"

To them I reply, "You've never had an older brother who's a party animal, have you?" The few times I invited myself in to sneak a snack from his refrigerator without proper invitation, I was hoisted by my own petard and was announced by screams from a half-naked woman who didn't expect to see a stranger in the kitchen. This was followed by a shout fest from a fully naked brother.

I learned the porch is a safe zone. There but not **there**, if you get the picture. Besides, not being entirely certain what time I was scheduled, I didn't want to wake him up early and have him in a foul mood for the entire day.

Six-thirty came and went, and so did the Breakfast Whipper.

By seven I was well into the magazine.

When I glanced at my watch again it was seven-fifty and still no sign of activity in the house. At eight-fifteen I got the strangest feeling that I had made a terrible mistake. The clinic must open very early and I had already missed my ride. I went to the garage and peeked in the window, but there sat the gleaming gold flake Barracuda with the fat racing tires. Obviously my brother was still home. He and that car were never more than a hundred yards from each other.

At eight-forty I began to worry. Maybe he was sick. Too much fun or the flu can do that to you, and perhaps he has just woken up, voided his body of whatever toxins through whatever means necessary, and collapsed back in bed after calling in sick. Obviously he couldn't contact me; I would have been on my way over here and cell phones had yet to be available.

I knew the clinic where he worked; it was about fifteen minutes away by car.

I waited until five past nine before I began knocking. Even sick, he should have the courtesy to step to the door and tell me to go home. After several attempts his angry sleep-ridden face appeared.

"What?!" he asked, sounding irritated, tired and confused all at the same time.

"I thought we were going to work today. It's almost quarter after nine. Are we going or what?"

"Dork," he scratched and yawned, "We're opticians. The shop doesn't open until ten. I show up at nine-fifty-five. Most days I don't even get up until about nine-thirty."

That was when I fell in love with the optical industry. Any occupation where you can party until one in the morning and **still** get a full eight hours sleep before work holds a special place in my heart.

"Wow," I thought, "I think I'm going to like this."

I didn't. I guess the balance scale of careers is a funny thing. People place so much weight on factors such as money, schedule, benefits, discounts. But the truth of the matter is, there's a big weight which falls on the other side - happiness. Most folks tend to see that weight as too small when seeking employment; that's why there are so many people working jobs they find dissatisfying. It's also why many people do volunteer work, choosing to spend their time doing something that makes them feel good, even if they get paid nothing. And some of us take jobs for low pay, just because we honestly enjoy the task at hand. We are the tomato pickin' pendejos of the world who are daily plucking truckloads of tomatoes and loving every minute of it.

But this wasn't picking tomatoes. This was basically factory work, running machines that cut and grind, and it was boring as all get-out.

My brother never found the job boring. But he worked the front of the clinic and dealt directly with the customers, leaving the backroom manufacturing work entirely to me after the first few weeks.

In those days, being a true optician was a trade. Many had fathers and grand-fathers, who had started in the business years before and owned dispensaries, from whom they'd learned the business.

There was a general respect for the trade as well. Opticians, like pharmacists, tended to wear white lab coats. The Ben Casey style worn by Vince Edwards, dentists and occasionally Bullwinkle J. Moose were fashionable and they were kept spotlessly white. This fostered the image in the patient's mind that opticians ranked somewhere below medical professionals, but above technicians in a quasi *Chiropractor-Anesthesiologist-School Nurse-ish* sort of way.

We who worked behind-the-scenes in manufacturing also wore lab coats, but ours were jacket-cut. Although white when issued, they gradually became stained from dyes, covered in the slurry produced while edging and grinding lenses and they lacked the Nehru collars, causing us to seem as though we were going for a Simon Bar Sinister couture.

```
    If you're asking, "Who are Bullwinkle and
Simon Bar Sinister," understand there was a
cartoon world long before Peter Griffin and Homer
Simpson that was filled with characters so
memorable that they transcend time, being iconic
in their appearance and rich in vocal textures.
Surprisingly, unlike today, very few of the
popular ones revolved around dysfunctional
families.
```

Months passed, and while I couldn't help learning about glasses, lenses and optics in general, I was keeping an eye on the want-ads for something closer to sales. And then, as luck would have it, my path got turned.

"I'm sick." It was my brother calling on my day off. "Can you go in for me?"

"To work?" I asked.

"No. Can you go in to the dentist for me? Dork."

"Why would I go to the dentist for you?" I loved it when he needed me because I knew he would play along.

"Look," he wheezed, "can you do it or not? I've got to let them know."

"Say 'please,'" I pushed.

"Please," he said.

"Say 'I'm a sick dork and I need your help.'"

"You're a sick dork, but I still need your help." Even sick he joked.

"OK, I'll do it," and added, "what time is your appointment?"

"Dork," he said and he hung up.

Later, at the clinic, I had the biggest urge to contact the dental department and have them call him and ask if he wanted to reschedule the appointment he missed.

CHAPTER FOURTEEN
Jacob and His Miracle

On that flu day, I moved out front. Leaving my old jacket behind like a cocoon, I slipped into the cool crisp whiteness of a dispensing jacket and began assisting patients with their selection of frames, lenses, contacts and associated accoutrements.

Looking back, I never believed I was involved in sales at the clinic, let alone Guiding. It could be that this seemed so different from every Retail Jungle I'd ever known that I couldn't comprehend that anyone would need a Guide's services. It may have been that I felt the prescribing doctor was the Guide, that in some way they "pre-guided" the patient during the exam. After all, wasn't that what a written prescription was, some kind of "map" for the patient? As far as the selection of eyeglass frames went, wasn't that just a matter of style?

So I didn't recognize anything close to the standard retail sales environment at the time, and as such, I pretty well assumed that I would return to the lab as soon as my brother resumed his health.

And then I performed a miracle.

Growing up, I remember Father Guido Sarducci on *Saturday Night Live*. I recall him complaining about St. Elizabeth Seton. He said, "To be made a saint in-a the catholic church, you have to have-a four miracles. That's-a the rules, you know. It's-a always been that-a. Four miracles, and-a to prove it. Well, this-a Mother Seton - now they could only prove-a three miracles. But the Pope -

he just waived the fourth one. He just waived it! And do you know why? It's-a because she was American. It's all-a politics. We got-a some Italian-a people, they got-a forty, fifty, sixty miracles to their name. They can't-a get in just cause they say there's already too many Italian saints, and this woman comes along with-a three lousy miracles. I understand that-a two of them was-a card tricks.."

Well, I'm definitely not a saint, but I've been involved with several miracles in my life, usually being the benign recipient of them. Most were major car wrecks where I walked away alive. This is the only one that I helped make happen for others.

Not thirty minutes after I showed up, the head of ophthalmology came to see me. He had with him two people who were holding on to each other in a manner that I can only describe as "in support." They walked side by side with each having an arm thrown around the other's back or shoulder. As they walked, they gently clasped open hand to open hand and seemed to lean into each other's frame. It seemed that at any second either one could collapse or the other would be responsible for keeping the former from crashing to the ground; they were each ready to fall, so they struggled on valiantly together, since neither seemed capable of making it alone.

Immediately the image made sense, because I had seen this posture at funerals.

"Oh, man," I said to myself, "somebody died."

It turns out it wasn't death, but it was tragedy, sorrow and loss of hope.

"These are the Nelsons," the doctor introduced us and I shook hands with each Nelson, "Their son Jacob is getting his bandages removed right now."

The words, "my brother has the flu" almost left my lips. But as I looked into their eyes I knew the Nelsons had somehow gotten the absolute worst end of the stick. I also could tell that whatever assistance I could give them they would get. They weren't wearing their hearts on their sleeves. They were all heart, and someone they loved was in a dire position.

At times like that, it's easy to see that you can summon up a better self, to make a better effort, and to be a better person.

"What do you folks need?" I replied and carefully listened.

Jacob had congenital aphakia. He had been born with clouded corneas and anomalies of the crystalline lenses of each eye, very similar to advanced cataracts. For the first six months of his existence, Jacob had been blind.

The weight of this news on the Nelsons was apparent.

Jacob had received cataract surgery, and the lenses of his eyes were excised, as was the treatment for cataracts at the time. Interocular implants were too new, and unavailable for several additional medical reasons.

The doctor continued, "We've completed binocular corneal transplants and the patches are coming off today. We've received the lenses for his glasses from the specialty manufacturing laboratory, but we need them mounted in a frame and the frame fit on little Jacob. Can you do that?"

I looked at the Nelsons, "Sure," I said, and saw probably two hundred pounds of weight leave their shoulders.

Optical manufacturing is simply precision manufacturing of glass and plastic. I had cut an edged lens, understood the principles, and was ready to go. But this was something beyond the usual.

Infants can't use regular eyeglass frames. They use what appears to be a miniature eyeglass frame front, and instead of ear pieces, a tiny elastic head harness system holds the glasses in place. I had seen these before when I helped with inventory, and was flabbergasted by the small size. The lens openings were, on the smallest model available, about the size of a dime for each eye.

To replace the lenses of the human eye requires about fifteen diopters of plus magnification power.

If this all sounds technical, let me make the image simpler for you. I was making glasses for Mr. Magoo. It just so happened that Mr. Magoo was, in this case, a six-month old baby. When I saw the lenses they looked like two bubbles. The edges of these un-cut blanks, as they are called, were already knife thin. Now my job was to take them from the size of about a quarter, and shape the edge down to the size and shape that would fit in the miniature frames.

There are machines that do this, and we had one. They use patterns to match the shape of the lenses to the shape of the frames. But in this case, the end size was just too small, even for the machines.

The Nelsons were seated in the waiting room, and I brought out the lenses and the frame to explain the predicament presented by the machine and its inherent size restrictions. Mr. Nelson had his arm around his wife shoulders.

"Any luck?" he said, looking up.

I was about to explain when Mrs. Nelson said something.

"He cries all the time," she said.

I just listened, I knew more was coming.

"He just cries and cries. I know he can't talk, and he can't see, and he's gone through so much, and he can only hear us when we speak. So we've been there every second we can, one or both of us, talking to him, singing to him, anything, just so he knows we're here."

"It's hard," added Mr. Nelson, voice almost cracking. "Maybe he will be OK?"

You may have been here. You may have been in a situation like this. If you have you would have realized as I did that there are going to be a world of disappointments and issues and failures that this child is going to face, but I'll be damned if I was going to be one of the contributors.

"Give me a few more minutes, it's just going to take me some more time because these are delicate to make," and I headed back to the lab.

The machines were useless, but there was another option. Occasionally, when someone broke a frame, it was possible to slightly alter the shape of the old lenses to fit a new frame. We did this with a hand wheel, a rotational grinding stone that took off a little material. If I was careful, I thought I could take the size down by hand for each lens.

Also, I needed to create a bevel on the edge of the lenses so the lenses would stay seated in the frame.

Also I needed to get the lenses aligned so they were straight when mounted.

Also, I needed to set the lenses in the frame for the measurements that the Doctor gave me.

That's a lot of "alsos."

About an hour later, I heard a baby-alarm going off. That continual crying sound that only infants seem to make which means, "I don't know who is in charge of life, but I am not happy with the conditions of the current situation," and Jacob was ushered table and all into our dispensary.

The patches had been removed and the Nelsons were overjoyed that all surgeries went as planned. Jacob was officially "light perceptive" and as such, had a good chance of seeing.

Vision in babies is debatable. By six months, it's generally agreed that a baby's vision is functioning pretty much as an adult's does. Unfortunately, Jacob hadn't had six months to prepare him for light, and he was making this strange event known.

Mr. and Mrs. Nelson tried to comfort him by making sounds and talking to him.

"He's cried his entire life," were the words I heard from the front while I did calculations.

It took me about an hour, but I carefully did what I planned and brought out a tiny little set of hand crafted "Magoozers" for the crying little Magoo. The doctor looked them over and said they looked great. Actually he was kind of impressed when he learned I had edged them by hand.

I fussed with the harness a little, adjusted straps and took a deep breath. I whispered over the raucous crying, "OK, here we go," while lowering the lenses over the eyes.

I went deaf.

I know this because all noise left the room and that could be the only explanation. I fiddled with one strap a little, then tested out my own voice to make certain that I hadn't accidentally killed the baby by doing something wrong with the straps. I knew they had a soft spot up there somewhere, but I wasn't certain if the pressure of a small elastic strip would injure the child, or possibly cause damage that would reduce his abilities to do taxes when he's fifty.

"Is he alright?" It was Mrs. Nelson breaking the silence.

"I think so," I said. "He's just kind of looking at me."

I did the only thing I could think of; I smiled really big at the little guy and said, "You OK there pal?" As I did it a new sound came out, somewhere between a giggle, a burp and a raspberry and all of a sudden little arms where attacking my face. I swear the kid was smiling while he continued to swat and squeal.

"Oh my God," and down went Mr. Nelson.

I've never had children of my own. I'm a proud step-dad, which means I get all the problems and benefits of being a biological parent, without the paternal bonds founded by eons of evolution. I also have the added pleasure, when the children do something so incredibly stupid that everyone sits back and shakes their heads, of being entitled to say, "they don't take after me." I'm a parent who sees children as they actually are, and not how I envision them. As such there is little that impresses me that children do, or don't do.

So when it comes to the idiosyncrasies of early development, it had always been difficult for me to understand the act of *imprinting*, what parents often feel when they witness the birth of their child. The fact that a first meeting between individuals is usually more memorable had, in my mind, always been attributable to the occasion being unique and singular, but in no other way special.

As I stood over Jacob, my perceptions changed.

I looked at him. He looked at me.

I looked at him. He looked at me.

I looked at him. He looked at me and smiled.

It wasn't until sometime later that one of the nurses told me babies smile when they have gas, and it probably had nothing to do with my presence. The baby had probably pooped.

But my heart and mind were forever changed by that moment, poop or no poop, because it wasn't Mrs. Nelson or Mr. Nelson, one of the nurses or even the doctors whom Jacob first laid eyes upon. It was me, and in his first glimpse of the entire universe I had made him smile. What I had just witnessed seemed as close to miraculous as anything I could imagine.

"Wow," I thought. "What an amazing job this is!" This thought was quickly followed by, "Wow, I hope his dad's OK."

From that point I was hooked on the rush of the optical field. Think about it. I was providing sight to the blind, helping patients see their world, their families and their friends. By working in this field I created enjoyment and fulfillment in the lives of people who were heretofore hindered.

But my calling was still to be a Professional Guide, so is it possible that there could be a Taoist satisfaction - a kind of yin and yang between the two careers?

The answer came as I was reading an article that noted and ranked optical shops against other retailers in malls across the United States. It turned out that due to the moderately substantial price of both an exam and a spectacles and/or a contact lens purchase, optical dispensaries created an above average sales-per-square-foot gross. Sales was a major part of the optical profession.

"No, it's not," Thomas quickly pointed out the next day as we drove to work together. He was still not recovered, but felt that the twenty-four hour bug had definitely passed its worst. The plan was for him to stay in the back of the lab, away from the patients and any possibility of contamination and for me to return to the front to assist the patients.

At this particular moment he was explaining why I was incorrect in my assumption.

"You really are a dork. It has nothing to do with sales," his tone sounded almost disgusted that I brought up any reference to the two occupations being interlaced. "In sales you try to push something on people; in optical we just fill the prescription the way doctor writes it. Besides, people don't want to buy glasses; they **have to** buy glasses. There's no salesmanship involved with giving someone something they have to buy."

As I listened to him ramble on, I simplified his position. He was trying to make it clear that opticians were Clerks, just filling the orders as requested.

"You're going to cause a lot of trouble around the clinic if you start treating patients like customers."

When the opportunity presented itself, I spent a minute with a few of the doctors in the lunchroom. When I asked for their opinions on sales, they also became a little agitated.

"You need to understand," they offered. "Many of the patients we see are on a limited budget, or only have state insurance to cover services and exams. They can't afford a lot of fancy extras or upgrades when it comes to eyeglasses. They will get offended if you try to pressure them into purchasing things they don't need. We don't want that." A murmur of agreement went around the room following the last comment. "Just get them what they need, or what the state allows if they have insurance."

It was decided. I was going to have to finish my few days out front, then probably return to the lab forever since I believed in a different way of handling patients when it came to eyewear. But as things often happen, a guiding hand was offered from an unexpected source. The Head of Ophthalmology, the doctor who had performed the surgeries on little Jacob, came in for some coffee while this was going on and had been listening to the debate. He cleared his throat in a particularly gentle manner he had, which silenced everybody in the room out of respect, and he let his opinion be known.

"Jacob Nelson," he began, and looked around the room for any one not recognizing the name of the clinic's recent premier poster child for outstanding healthcare, "is doing wonderfully well. I have a note here from the Nelsons thanking the hospital and this young man for his kindness, warmth, skills and professionalism."

You could have heard a pin drop as he went on.

"I can't imagine Jeff suggesting anything that's not in the best interest of a patient."

Later, Thomas was still upset.

"I hope you're happy with yourself" he said, "Now we have to hire a new tech for the lab; the doctors want you full time in the dispensary."

It lasted for four months, my brother and I working side by side, but too many chiefs and not enough Indians precipitate a rain dance. Ours was over who should pick up lunch each day. He stamped his feet and said it was my responsibility, I stamped mine and said it wasn't; and by the time the storm had ended I had quit.

They say working with family is like working with bees; you need a lot of respect and chances are you'll still get stung. Thomas, over the past few months had said some things that stung, and so did I. It became obvious that working together was never going to prove practical. Parting was not an issue, since I had taken the job only as a temporary measure, and now he had hired another person to run the lab. We ate lunch that last day, after I went to pick it up for the last time, and hugged hard. It was a Wednesday.

By the way, Wednesdays are great days to quit, especially midday. You get most of the week to recover, look for jobs and rest. By the following Monday, you're refreshed and ready for new adventures.

CHAPTER FIFTEEN
Of Wants and Needs

The help-wanted ad said, "Salesman wanted for large optical retail chain," so I applied.

Unlike the clinic, there was no mistaking the direction of peddling at these offices. Large newspaper advertisements boldly made claims to the consumer about low prices. The locations where strewn with fashion posters bearing designer's names. Thousands of eyeglass frames covered every wall along with huge boards of sunglasses, contact lens supplies, accessories and other related merchandise.

The Regional Manager interviewed me and was impressed with my knowledge of optical manufacturing, but when it came to my experience with customers, he felt I was still a novice and said so.

"You've only dispensed and sold eyewear for a few months, and this was at a clinic?"

"Yeah, I was working with my brother while learning the trade. I was out front for the last few months selling and working with customers," I replied.

"What was your A.S.P.?" he asked.

"My what?" I was confused.

I always get confused by acronyms. We found a dog one summer and my mother asked me to call the animal shelter and see if anyone had reported it missing. It took me over a dozen calls, and while the folks at the animal shelter had no reports of missing pets, the AARP knew several people who would take it and the NAACP said they were interested in helping as well, but only after I explained it was a **black** lab.

"Your A.S.P.," he repeated, "Your Average Sale Per customer."

"Well," I wanted to be honest, "we had a lot of insurance patients and a lot of state aid patients."

He picked up his coffee cup, reading over some figures, eyes down on the page as if he was listening only as obligated. "Certainly, I understand. We've tried to hire people from that sector before, but they aren't familiar with high end sales and…"

"Around eight hundred dollars," I said.

The cup stopped and the eyes popped up off the page he was scanning, "What?"

"What?" I asked.

"What did you say?" he asked.

"I said around eight hundred dollars."

"Per customer?" He watched me.

"Per eye." He either missed or ignored my humor.

"No," he put the coffee cup down and became very serious as if he was explaining the dangers of matches to a toddler, "I mean, if you take the last ten customers who bought glasses from you, and added up how much they paid in total, and then you divided that number by ten you get the average amount that each customer paid."

"Is that how that works?" He didn't hear my sarcasm. "I understand math, and I understand how to figure out an average," I said. "I was confused because you seemed perplexed by my answer."

"Eight hundred dollars is high," he said flatly.

"Compared to what?"

"Compared to the industry," he said. "Most people who need glasses buy one, sometimes two, pairs. The average sale is around one hundred and fifty dollars a pair, without insurance. With insurance, the average customer pays about fifty dollars in addition to what's covered by their insurance. Patients covered under state programs usually skip upgrades all together. We sell and promote higher-end merchandise, multiple-pair sales and designer frames, but even our best sales people only average around three hundred dollars per pair. You're telling me you worked at a clinic, where you saw a high number of patients that had state or private insurance and your average sale was eight hundred dollars? That's impossible."

"Actually, it was pretty easy once I understood how to guide my customers," I said.

He watched me, and I knew that the papers he was reviewing and the coffee in his cup were forgotten.

So I paused, because I love taking that pause, knowing that they are hooked and that my Tour, this time an *Application Tour*, was about to begin. And I explained about lesson #16.

Lesson #16 – It is easier to sell to someone who "needs" than it is to sell to someone who "wants."

This is so basic a concept that entire sales training programs have been based around teaching and developing the ability to comprehend and utilize it. Companies spend thousands of dollars annually to have their sales forces trained on this concept, without it ever being written as simply as I've stated for you right now.

Yet, it is almost incomprehensible to the average salesperson. It really takes a Professional Guide to put it to use.

I became aware of the how this worked during those last four months at the clinic. By being given free rein to work out front with the patients, I was able to see if there was a way of increasing sales while not offending those I was permitted to assist.

As a Guide, I understood that my Tour would revolve around the Optical Jungle, but that wasn't enough. I understood about prescriptions, lenses, curves and everything technically pertinent to manufacturing functional eyewear for a patient. On the nuts and bolts, I was a Certified Specialist. But I didn't understand my Tourists, and that was step number one.

By the way, you don't have to stop in order to learn, change, evolve or re-group when you're a Guide. You can change your Tours daily, continually tweaking and improving as you go along.

Imagine a safari guide in an actual jungle. Every day new vines and plants are growing and shifting. As one path grows over, another might reveal itself. This new path might prove more rewarding for tourists, who get to glimpse flora and fauna which have never before been accessible. Change, and the ability to explore new paths and see new aspects of the same Retail Jungle, is all part of the lure of becoming a Guide. It's all part of the adventure.

As part of re-grouping and looking for new paths, I spoke with Tourists who had previously experienced the optical Jungle. It was easy to tell who they were because they had old eyeglasses when they arrived. This is good advice for any retailer: if you want to know what changes you should make, don't ask your staff, ask your customers.

I asked one of my patients, "Mrs. Henner, can I ask you a question?" Mrs. Henner was ninety-four and one of those women with a remarkably quick wit that prove men are God's afterthought. He just invented man first because we were simpler.

"Is it about sex?" she asked me flat out.

"No Ma'am," I blushed.

"Good. Then what can I help you with?" She didn't miss a beat.

I looked at the frames she had selected and the prescription before me. "How long have you been wearing glasses?"

"You should never ask a woman her age, dear," she admonished.

"I'm not." I already knew her age from her chart. "I was just wondering how many times you've purchased glasses over the years."

"Well," she seemed to be calculating, "I've been wearing them since I was," she paused, "young." She smiled and continued, "I would say this might be, oh, the fifteenth time I've purchased new glasses."

That seemed reasonable, so I went on. "From every record I have here, these are your only pair, is that right?"

"Not really. I have an old pair that used to be Mr. Henner's before he passed on. I keep those around for an emergency, in case I break my regular pair."

That seemed strange, since I found it hard to believe that Mr. Henner's prescription would be accurate for her, but I guess it was close enough that she could use it in a pinch.

"What I was wondering was, why don't you buy an extra pair so you have another to use as a backup, or as something for a change of style?" I asked.

She looked at me as if I was an imbecile. "Because, I don't *want* to buy another pair. I only have one set of eyes; I only *need* one pair of glasses."

A moment of clarity came over me as she said that. I saw *want* and *need* balancing on a scale. Take *want* off, and the scale never changes. *Want* is nothing. It's an ethereal concept that has no real weight in deciding if someone should make a purchase.

Need does. *Need* gives us the green light to sign the charge slip, take the money from our wallet or write the check.

Once I had that sorted out, I was able to gain more perspective on the influence of *want*.

Want steers our decision of what to purchase to satisfy our needs.

Need **drives** a Tourist; "You *need* something, go find it."

Want **steers** Tourists on a Tour; when they come to a fork in the road, *want* decides which path they should take.

***Want* is a direction, *need* is an impetus.**

Now, in every class I have taken, book I have read or suggestion I have heard from sales trainers, when it comes to "how to sell" they will start telling you how consumers purchase items on impulse. This *impulse buying* accounts for most of the last minute purchases, up-grades, add-ons, accessories and bling that make up a high-end sale.

They are wrong.

Let's look at it from a different angle. Make a list in your mind right now of all the things you want. Fill it up with electronics, cars, jewelry, clothes, sporting goods - matter of fact, list everything your heart has ever dreamed of. Those are your wants.

Now ask yourself: why are those not yours right now? The easy answer is lack of money. But there are some items you may have listed which really don't cost that much money at all - perhaps a new set of shoes, or a CD. What's stopping you from getting those today?

It's lack of enough *need*. You don't really need it yet, you feel you need your money more. Until need reaches a critical level, you can do without.

Or, think of it as a meal. You've just eaten a great dinner and you're full when the waiter asks, "dessert?" You quickly respond, "no thank you." You do that because you're no longer hungry, you've lost the need for more food and you won't purchase, prepare or eat more food again until the need arises. For some of us that's several hours and for some it's several minutes, but the fact remains - you're not going to eat again until you feel the need.

If you're asked "dessert?" and say "you bet!" it's not because you **want** a piece of twelve-layer Bavarian crème torte, it's because you've convinced yourself you **need** a piece of twelve-layer Bavarian crème torte, and you can't leave the table, your needs satisfied, without it.

Simply wanting something isn't enough. So, the concept of *impulse buying* doesn't really fly. You won't buy something just because you want it. You've got to be convinced on some level that you truly need it.

Ron Popeil is probably saying how wrong I am, since he seems to have made an industry out of the impulse buy, but I think he would see my side of this. The fact is, a lot of people actually need a rotisserie cooker, a pocket fishing system and a rhinestone and stud setter. They just didn't realize they needed it until they were presented with the product.

Fifty years ago, nobody needed a cell phone and internet access. Then someone invented it, presented it and marketed it. Pretty soon almost everybody realized they needed it.

The need was always there, it was just undiscovered - like a new path through a Jungle. Once it's discovered, Tourists start to realize they needed it all along, but the Guide needs to introduce it.

Currently, the US is in a bit of a recession. Some folk would call it severe. Unemployment is approaching ten percent; banks and financial institutions are going under or charging rates which they will be ashamed of when the world rights itself. But in the midst of this havoc, sales are still happening. Economists everywhere cry that average citizens have cut back, that they have stopped frivolous spending.

While all this appears reasonable and educated in the way it's presented, it seems obvious that it's not a matter of spending less. It's simply a matter of a change in **needs** which doesn't include immediate purchases.

Everyone I know still **wants** to go out to eat, to purchase big screen TVs and new sneakers for the children. But the economy, the government and the world media has squelched the urgent **need** to make these purchases right now. Currently, everyone has decided that the primary need is to save. Yet purchases still go on and while retail sales are down, sales are still being made.

Want is still incredibly high, but **need** is the determining factor in purchasing.

If you're still in doubt, here's the lock: children. I've asked everyone I know who has children why they became a parent and a hundred percent say, "I had a child because I **needed** it to make my life complete." People who have the ability can have children any time they want, but they make the commitment to try when the vague **want** for children becomes a specific **need** for a child. That is the story of every child of a planned pregnancy in existence.

```
Of course I, myself, am one of what is
affectionately known as a group of children
called "whoops babies." We are the byproduct of
fulfillment of another more primal and urgent
need; we know this was a definite need, because
the initial vague want included more preparation
time and probably a stop at a drug store.
```

As I grasped the larger picture of wants and needs, I began talking with patients at the clinic more; taking more time reviewing what they already knew about the eyewear they had previously purchased; and looking for what they needed to know but had yet to learn about new frames, lenses, treatments and accessories to best fulfill their needs.

This led to the next lesson:

Lesson #17 – Tourists don't know what they don't know. It is the duty of Guides to inform them of what's available and what they may need, and to uncover needs they didn't know they had.

This is another simple concept taught by sales trainers to thousands yet never summed up so clearly.

```
    If you're wondering whether this book was
worth what you paid, these last two lessons cost
one company I knew over twenty-five thousand
dollars to hear from a lecturer.
```

At the clinic, everybody, even I, thought we understood **need**. After all, I was a trained optician and I should be aware of every patient's needs. I didn't and I wasn't.

Patients need glasses to see. But any glasses, even the least expensive pairs, if manufactured according to the parameters of the prescription, will allow someone to see. I thought the need would be vision; usually it wound up to be so much more than that.

In the optical industry there are dozens upon dozens of options from which the patient can choose. Each of these options make the eyewear function or perform slightly differently.

Multiple options are available in every retail environment. If you work in a clothing shop, you have accessories that could completely change an outfit from formal to informal. In a restaurant, changing sides and condiments can completely change the aspect of the entrée. In an electronics store, purchasing a video gaming system just opens the door to the hundreds of games and accessories available to immerse you in the gaming experience.

My brother had explained about these optical options when I began working out front. He said, "These are all the available extras that the patients can add to their glasses. Don't force anything on them; just ask them if they would like any of these options. If they say yes, mark the order and here's the price list to figure out the charges." He had made these variables sound like more a nuisance than a possibility. I knew right away that he was missing the boat.

Many of the options were wonderful. We had specialty lens materials which were thinner and lighter, and some materials were extremely safe and protected the eyes against accidental impacts. There were even several photochromic materials which would darken when you went into sunlight, then clear when you returned indoors. Colored tints, prescription sunglass lenses and specialty coating could make your lenses appear as mirrors, or mask reflection to a point where the lenses seemed to disappear. Add to this over a thousand different frames made of every material you could imagine in every style, shape and color possible.

I had been following the guidelines my brother had set forth. I would fill the prescription, and offer all these wonderful add-ons, hearing around a thousand replies of "thank you, but no thank you." But after that exchange with Mrs. Henner, I changed my approach.

"Mrs. Henner, would you do me a favor? I've got a new frame that just came in. I haven't showed it to anyone, but I'd like your opinion." Going to the back, I returned with a crimson frame that was as bright as a stop light at midnight.

"Here," I handed it to her, "try this on."

When she put on that frame her whole face blossomed. At ninety-four, she had naturally lost some of her youthful color, but this frame acted like rouge on her cheeks.

"Oh my, I look like a movie star," she smiled as she turned her head and watched herself in the desk mirror.

"OK, now let me show you something else." I took a sample lens from the drawer that had been coated with anti-reflective coating and held it over one eye for her. "Can you see how this treatment gets rid of those annoying lens reflections and lets everyone see your eyes?"

"Yes, but, oh dear, who wants to see my eyes with all these wrinkles and lines?" She seemed vexed.

"Hang on now," I continued, "we can put a little soft rose coloring into the lenses." I showed her a sample. "And we can fade the color so it appears that you have a light natural blush on the eyes. Plus, if we go with a no-line bifocal we can get rid of the lines made by your glasses too."

She looked shocked. "What do you mean no-line bifocals?"

I stopped, because then it just hit me, I was already giving a Tour and I hadn't even realized it myself.

"Mrs. Henner," I said, and then I paused, enjoying the anticipation, "we are going to design you some glasses, and they will be the most wonderful glasses you've ever had. I'm going to ask you some questions, and it's OK if you don't know the answer, but the more information you give me, the better I can do my job.

We're going to create glasses that, of course, fulfill your optical needs. But they will do more than that. They will fulfill every demand you have for vision, every whim you have for style and every need you have for function and performance."

"This sounds exciting," she said.

"Honestly," and I meant it, "it is for me too."

It sounds easy, but that was just one person. Mrs. Henner's sale ended up consisting of three pairs of glasses with a ticket of slightly over fifteen hundred dollars, which she paid with a check and a hug. I know she is no longer in this world, but God bless the Mrs. Henners everywhere. Elderly women with class and humor are an example to all of us that people may, like good wine, age wonderfully and bring pleasure into the lives of those who imbibe.

I would miss her. Repeat customers make the life of a Guide fun. We enjoy seeing those we've helped return again and again. And you learn fast there are only three reasons people return to your location: to purchase, to praise or to complain.

At the clinic, I was somewhat assured that my patients were going to make some purchase. We did our job competently, so there were few complaints. Praise usually came in the form of Christmas cards and occasionally a batch of chocolate chip cookies with a scribbled note.

No one meandered through a clinic to waste a few minutes, peeking in and out of exam rooms announcing to those who inquired, "I was just looking."

This fact dawned on me when the first retail customer walked through the door on my first day at my new store. I had passed the interview, been hired and was positioned on the sales floor. As she entered, I was greeted with a simple announcement:

"I'm just looking," she said.

"For what?" I was curious, having never encountered this previously as a greeting.

"Nothing in particular," she gave me a weird look which I interpreted as a sign that I was invading her space somehow by responding to her statement.

I just stood there politely and watched.

"I'm browsing," she said in a more authoritarian tone.

That was obvious, so I tried to assure her it was alright to proceed with her agenda.

"Nothing wrong with browsing," I told her and smiled.

She picked up a frame and tried it on, then another and surveyed her reflection in a nearby mirror. She noticed I was still there and turned on me abruptly.

"Look," her voice had a slight edge to it, "I'm not going to steal anything if that's what you're concerned about."

I hadn't been, until she made that comment. Funny how an idea never pops into your head until someone vocalizes it, and then you can't seem to get it out of your thoughts.

"I wouldn't assume you were; you don't look like someone who steals." I was smiling as I said it, yet she still seemed nervous. I tried to calm her with a little more information. "I'm just hanging around in case you have any questions."

"I don't," she put the frames down. "I was just looking." And with that she abruptly left the shop.

The office was in a strip mall next to a women's clothing store. There were several to-go food restaurants, a jewelry store, a large chain bookstore and an electronics store as well.

I watched her as she left. She meandered down to the women's clothing shop and entered. About twenty minutes later I saw her exit a store, parcels in hand, make her way to her car and leave. This same scenario was repeated dozens of times by different people over the course of my first two weeks. As I started paying attention to the shopping patterns of people who frequented the mall, it became very clear that while shoppers may have a specific destination in mind, they were more than willing to burn some time cycling in and out of several different stores before procuring the item they originally set out to acquire. Usually, I would see people heading back to their cars with packages from several of the retailers in the mall.

Thursday night, after I left work, I headed to the grocery store. I needed to pick up a few things. On my list were the usual staples: milk, eggs, bread, cheese. I'm from a state known for dairy and a lack of it in some form for more than one meal makes me nervous.

At the checkout lane I looked over the groceries of the person ahead of me and began taking inventory.

Tampons, hairclips, chocolate ice cream, aluminum foil, gum and some parker house rolls. I thought over those items while the cashier swiftly passed each of them over the scanner and the bagger scooped them into "paper or plastic."

My first thought was about how eclectic a list that seemed, but I hadn't seen any list. It appeared that she was one of those individuals with the gift of being able to remember what she needed at the grocery store without a shopping list.

I've never been one of those people. I'm one of the people who make two trips every time I attempt it. You can see us in the ten-items-or-less line at the store with a single can of pumpkin pie filling muttering over and over again, "Pie filling. How did I forget pie filling?"

As I reviewed her items I tried to determine what were the items needed to precipitate the trip. Tampons seemed an obvious guess and that might explain the ice cream. I've got stepdaughters now and understand that there is some magic numbering in the sizes of tampon boxes which end up with exactly enough so you don't need to go to the store for more halfway through, but magically use the last one at just the right second so you can go twenty-eight days without remembering to tell your stepfather you need more, just so you can start screaming from the bathroom as he steps through the front door: "Oh my God, we're out of tampons! Dad, can you run to the store? And don't forget to get some chocolate ice cream!"

Maybe, the whole problem could be corrected if some executive from a hot dog bun corporation would take over the tampon industry. Then no matter how hard you tried to purchase the exact amount you require, there would always be two extra floating around.

Gum seemed a long shot. It's one of those items you need only when you realize you're out and have a social event imminently close at hand.

Or it may have been the aluminum foil and parker house rolls. Perhaps she was having someone over for dinner and was baking something that needed foil for the cover, and the rolls went with the meal. It could even be someone special. I looked at her hand and there was no wedding ring.

Maybe, it was someone really special. A guy she met and was inviting over to her house for a home cooked meal, complete with rolls. Her hair would look just perfect with the new hair clips. She would serve chocolate ice cream for dessert because everyone knows that chocolate releases the same chemicals in the body as love and he would have new deep feelings for her. Then she would chew a stick of gum to be certain their first kiss was minty and fresh.

I glanced back over at the tampons.

"Better enjoy the kiss, buddy, it ain't going any further," I thought.

As the fantasy left my mind, I looked over my own cart: milk, eggs, bread and cheese, plus some extras.

The cheese was expensive. That's a funny way to describe cheese, by price over taste, but it was. It happened to be a nice wedge of Romano which I have come to enjoy shredded over pasta, on a salad, or just eaten in small cuts with a glass of good wine.

```
A glass of wine, a little cheese, some good
bread and fresh fruit is a dinner I can't
recommend enough. It is a meal for the spirit; it
is food for thought.
```

The cheese was eighteen dollars a pound, and this little wedge was just under a pound.

The basket also held a two-pack of sixty-watt bulbs, a pack of twenty disposable razors and a bottle of cold bottled water from a case adjacent to the checkout stand.

I had picked up the items without much real thought, but now I began looking for underlying needs to assess the validity of my hypothesis on needs and wants.

Did I need the light bulbs? Yes. I just had not realized it until I saw them; they were an undiscovered need. The bulb over my front porch had burnt out weeks ago, but I had forgotten until seeing the bulbs in the store jogged my memory. I only needed one, but bulbs seem to come in packs of two like *Ross's Peanut Buster Cups©*, so I was purchasing two.

The razors? They had to be in impulse purchase - a simple matter of want. Unlikely. I shave because I must. I'm not a beard man. I often attempt to grow one and make it to two weeks before I get a fit of scratching, which ends the experiment every time. Razors are a need, but twenty? Then I remembered that they were on sale, and noticing that I was saving twenty percent; my logical brain had simply bumped the need to the front of the line. "Why wait?" it had said, "You're going to need to buy them next week anyway."

Lesson #18 – Need can be augmented by value; the better the value, the more urgent the need. This phenomenon can even go into overdrive creating needs that exceed financial resources. This explains the entire reason for the rise of credit cards.

That left the water. I was about to put it back in the case when my throat said "Hey! What are you thinking?" and a dry cough escaped me as a reminder that I was parched. The water was purchased and didn't even make it to the car as I downed the entire bottle once outside the store.

No. Everything I purchased, on some level or another I had needed. Even the cheese I had needed, and even at the price.

While there were cheddars, jacks, blues and a dozen types of goat cheese which would all have satisfied my penchant for cultured dehydrated curds, it was the Romano that I settled on because of a quick tour offered by the Cheese Guide at Global Bazaar, where I shop.

"Eating or cooking?" he asked.

"Shopping," was the response I came up with.

"Naturally, you're here," and by stating the obvious he clarified his question.

"Eating, I guess." I had picked up a nice aged cheddar and was enjoying the aroma even through the wrapper. Cheddars always have a nice warm smell to me, like a fireplace on a rainy day.

"May I see your basket?" he asked politely.

"Sure." He scanned the milk, eggs and razors which were the only items so far represented.

"Hang on a second." He unwrapped a large block of something on the back counter. "Do you like wine?"

"I'm Italian," I said and felt so stereotypical, as if I had said that every Englishman automatically loves stout and every Polish person automatically loves good bread.

> They do, by the way, but it's very stereotypical to announce it. It is the same with Italians and wine.

Either way, he was too polite to point out my assumptive comment.

Handing me a small wedge of the golden heaven he had cut, I put the sample in my mouth.

"Don't chew it!" It was like a command, so my jaw halted at mid crunch. "Just let it kind of melt on your tongue."

The sliver began to dissolve and evolve.

"Can you taste that? A kind of nutty flavor? It's balanced against the salt. There's a kind of graininess on the tongue."

He described it perfectly.

"Ok, now chew. Slowly," he directed and I followed.

I've come to the conclusion that for the most part, people just don't eat correctly. Not the usual, you're-not-obeying-the-food-pyramid nutritional incorrectness, but the eating-way-too-fast mistake.

> Recently, I had a great lunch at a nice restaurant. I thought carefully over each selection, asked the Restaurant Guide for advice and suggestions without a preference to anything specific, but seeking items that would complement each other during the meal. I became a complete Tourist to the Guide's skill, ordering portions that were small, but interesting and exotic. In the end I had spent over ninety minutes savoring and enjoying every bite, every single mouthful, and I realized I had eaten much less, yet enjoyed the experience much more than any meal I had

eaten in years. By really concentrating on getting the most out of the experience, probably any experience, you can reach an almost Zen-like state of enjoyment. It's the benefit of true Tourism in the hands of capable Guides - complete bliss.

The Cheese Guide was a Pro. The mixture melted into tastes of rich butter, warm sunshine and the recalled contentment of my early years dining in my Italian Grandma's kitchen. (Grandma-Pasta, my mother's mother; not to be confused with my father's mother, Grandma-Rutabaga.)

"You have a good wine to go with that?" he asked.

"I've got a nice Soave at home and some peaches I picked up the other day. Nice and ripe." I said. "Plus, I'm picking up a fresh loaf of sourdough."

"Good, that's great. Don't chill the wine too much; you'll want to get the bite of the acidity up and over-chilling tends to cut the flavor. Make sure you get the heavy crust round loaf. You'll need the bread for balance." This guy knew what he was talking about.

It hadn't even occurred to me to ask how much it was when he handed me the wedge. When he noticed me looking at the price he put it in perspective.

"That's really good cheese," he said, and I nodded in agreement. "It's ok to buy yourself good cheese. You deserve that on your table. Besides, you saved money on those razors."

I put it in my basket and didn't think about price again.

Lesson #19 – Tourists tend to believe they are undeserving of occasional luxury, even in the simplest of purchases. It is the duty of a Guide to let them know that whatever their decision, "whether they deserve it or not" should not be in the equation.

Later, in the checkout lane, I asked myself if I really needed a seventeen-dollar piece of cheese. As I thought over the past week, the growing pains associated with a new job and the lingering flavor of the sample, there wasn't any doubt. Yes, I absolutely needed this seventeen-dollar piece of Romano.

Dinner Thursday night was fantastic.

Friday morning, as I was thinking about my experience with the Cheese Guide, a thought started picking away at me. I was "just looking" when I hit the cheese counter and I ended up buying a wedge of cheese that was almost as expensive as everything else in my basket combined. The Cheese Guide had given me a sample, which was a hundred percent recommendation, but he also knew facts I didn't. He understood the taste and made a great recommendation. He represented himself as the Expert. And, he gave me permission to indulge myself.

"Aw, come on" I said going over it again and again, "it can't be THAT easy. Heck, that makes sales almost appear - **simple**."

# CHAPTER SIXEEN
Training the Guides

She walked in from the *Skirt Shed*™ next door and had her purse in one arm and a purchase in the other. As she stepped inside, the greeting seemed to fall from my mouth.

"Hello. I'm Jeff, and I'm here to help." It sounded pretentious and planned, even to me. But I remember reading somewhere that asking a question that can be answered with a yes or no tends to close the conversation. To stay completely away from that, I had decided on a statement as being the best strategy for a greeting. The fact that I was there to help, as I had announced, seemed a good simple statement.

She smiled, and walked over to the sunglasses. It was a beautifully sunny day, and I noticed she wasn't wearing any when she entered.

"Here's something cool," I said as I handed her a nice pair of sunglasses from the rack. "But don't put them on. Just look through the lenses from the back while holding them away from your face."

"Ah, I'm just looking," she said right on cue. Ok, time to see if this will work.

"That's what I figured," I said, then went on. "So I thought you'd like something cool to look at. Isn't that the point of looking?" It was a rhetorical question, but she actually nodded in agreement, so I continued.

"Now look through the lenses at all the other sunglasses." She followed my instructions to the letter. This was going to be fun if it worked.

"Now turn the glasses ninety degrees so the frame is going up and down instead of back and forth, and watch all the lenses on the sunglass board." I instructed. When she turned the sunglasses in her hand, she began laughing.

"That's cute!" she said. "How did you do that?"

Honesty is the best policy. "Careful placement," I said.

"No," she spoke to me while she kept turning the glasses back and forth. "How do you make the letters blink?"

I knew what she was trying to ask because it had taken me a few minutes to arrange the sunglass board this morning. About half the sunglasses the store carried had polarized lenses. By strategically laying out the sunglasses with polarized lenses, I had spelled 'HI' in big block letters on the board. After I filled in the remaining board space with non-polarized sunglasses, the board looked completely full.

Polarized sunwear has a unique property. When you oppose the axis against other polarized lenses, as she was doing by turning the pair in her hand, all light is blocked and other polarized lenses you're looking at appear to blink dark black. To her it appeared the board had electronically blinked 'HI' every time she turned the glasses. Without a pair of polarized sunglasses to demonstrate the effect, the board just looked like an ordinary board of sunglasses.

"Wow!" she said.

That simple trick opened the door. I gave her a taste, and I was the Expert, having known something she hadn't.

The pair she bought, which looked really great with the new blouse she had purchased next door, cost one-hundred-and-seventy-five dollars. She scheduled a contact lens exam for later that week too. It had been only a little over a year since her last exam, but she liked my approach and my office, and her previous doctor had not sent her a reminder. When she returned, it was for a compete eye exam, new contact lenses, eyeglasses and a set of prescription polarized glasses to use when she wasn't wearing her contacts. All together, the total sale came to just under twelve hundred dollars.

That's when I figured it out. "Just looking" is a truncated sentence. What most people really would say if they didn't have control was this:

"I'm just looking for something to buy. I'm probably going to buy something, somewhere, today. I have some limits, but I am willing to vary those limits as soon as I see something I need. It can be something I need to live, or it can be something I need to make me happy. But if I don't find something I need here, I'll just mosey around until I do find something I need - and then I'll buy it."

My system was simple:

- Find some way for the Tourist to sample - touch it, see it, hold it, whatever worked.
- Be the Expert. Know something interesting about every item you sell that makes it unique and fun.
- Help Tourists uncover their needs, be the Guide.
- Give Tourists permission to indulge themselves.

It was work, trying to figure out something interesting about every item, but in a few weeks I had a good handle on everything. Every "just looking" was met with a "Great! Let me show you something!" The more needs I uncovered, the more recommendations I made and the more sales followed.

After a few weeks the Regional Manager stopped by the location and took me out to lunch.

"I've got the sales figures from the store for the past month," he said. "Do you know what your A.S.P. is?"

"That's my average sale per customer. Didn't we go through this when you hired me?"

"No," again he missed my humor. "I mean do you know what you're A.S.P. is for this past month?"

"Not really. I know we're supposed to keep those figures handy, but actually I've been busy selling glasses and contacts," I said.

"Four hundred and seventeen," he looked at me unblinking.

I was floored. I would have thought it much higher than that.

"I'm sorry, really. Four hundred and seventeen per patient?"

He cracked a smile.

"No," he said, "per eye." As he turned the calculation sheet around I saw the number highlighted and circled, eight hundred and thirty four dollars A.S.P. was next to my name.

"We'd like you to run an office. Are you up for it?" he asked.

Wage follows responsibility. Running a retail location naturally pays more than working a retail location. A General Manager is responsible for many aspects of profit and loss, inventory control and business development. I discovered that all this responsibility comes out to slightly less than ten thousand dollars a year additional in your pay envelope.

"But, you're a Manager now." The emphasis in my Regional Manager's voice assured me that I was obviously missing the point. The numbers on the paper assured me that I wasn't.

He saw he needed to make a clarification. "There's also a year-end bonus which can be substantial, depending on profitability of the location. If you can keep costs down, you can qualify for several thousand dollars more at the end of the year."

I was skeptical, but he assured me that if I could keep payroll and other costs in line, the bonus would be there. Everything looked reasonable, so I accepted the position.

Within three weeks I understood why the previous Manager had left. This store was a disaster: a microscopic outlet attached to an even more microscopic doctor's office in a retail mall. This sounds ideal for overhead, and it would have been if sales where there - but they weren't. The location also had stiff competition. Three larger, more fashionable and upscale optical retailers, one known for their professionalism, one for their quick service "In About Fifty-Three Minutes" and one known for their inventive deals (we give you three pairs of glasses, two pair of contacts, ALL for $132.97!) were all present.

In a world of value, service and price, I was the man without a country.

The one saving grace for us was location. By some twist of fate we were located right next to the movie theatres at the mall's main entrance. This meant we received more walk-by traffic than the competition - a fact that was pointed out by the Regional Manager when he handed me the keys.

He was right, to a point. We did get a great deal of walk-by traffic. Usually it was potential customers who "walked by" our location to the competition.

Because it was a mall store, we had the added benefit of "mall store hours," which meant a seven-day work week, from nine to nine. Include opening and closing time, and we needed a warm body for almost ninety hours a week. There was a strict "no overtime except during emergencies" policy, which meant I was forced to have three fulltime staff members. Currently, three fulltime staff members plus a Manager put this store's payroll percentage so far out of whack that I soon realized it would be impossible to achieve a profit margin with any possibility of a bonus.

I needed a game plan and I needed it fast.

When a Guide is faced with deterrent issues, she changes the Tour. The ability to adapt the Tour is one of the best tools a Professional Guide possesses.

You can adapt the Tour for different types of Tourists. For example, if you work as a Clothing Guide and are getting bombarded by younger Tourists, you could lean more heavily on younger styles in your suggestions. In this way you truly are a Guide, simply steering the Tourist toward more appropriate selections.

As a Restaurant Guide, you may change your Tour to reflect new options and choices which are available only for a limited time, such as daily specials offered by the restaurant.

Adaptation to changes in availability, environment and the customer are often necessary to succeed, or to overcome what appears to be the insurmountable.

As I examined my situation, I began to realize this was something different. A quick survey of the competition proved that, while our location wasn't the least expensive, we weren't out of line for the mall's clientele. Demographically, we should be able to compete.

The store could use a good cleaning, a little paint and an eye towards foot traffic flow; but we were presentable. There was nothing that wouldn't be solved with a little spit, polish and some elbow grease. This is a small, but in no way trivial, matter which many retailers overlook. A ceiling tile discolored due to water damage, or a spot on the carpet, can turn off potential Tourists.

My wife calls this the "dirty restroom effect." She can need to use a bathroom so bad that her legs are locked at the knees and she's hopping around the car. Within ten seconds of stopping at a gas station and finding out their restroom is somewhat less than sparkling, she'll be back in the car announcing, "I can wait."

The same holds true for retail. Whatever type of store you work in, you should view it freshly each day, as if it was your first introduction to the location, and ask yourself, "Would I shop here?"

So I planned on improving the appearance to best reflect a location where I would make a purchase. Then I thought about the overall situation. When I looked at it from the top, only two reasons could account for the poor performance: the Guides were incapable, or the Tourists were not interested in the Tours offered.

I needed to train staff and I needed to draw business. I began by evaluating the staff to see exactly where I could help. Training is a form of help or assistance, since it does absolutely no good to attempt to train someone who is uninterested in learning. That's another gem many retail companies overlook. Thousands are spent putting together rigorous training programs for staff who would rather not improve. It's similar to the Salem Witch Hunts where they would ask someone accused of witchery if they were a witch. If they answered "no," they were tortured or hung for not admitting to witchery. Faced with that reward for truth, people agreed to lie to stay alive.

Asking an employee with poor performance if they would like training to improve their skills is the same type of question. Do you really think most employees are not smart enough to understand that saying, "No, I just want to continue performing poorly" will end their employment?

So everyone says "yes" to training when it's offered. But finding out who can really benefit from it, improve because of it and will use the skills they have learned is a true sifting process. At this point in my career I hadn't yet figured that out, so I decided to train everybody. Besides, it was only three people.

CHAPTER SEVENTEEN
Price, Service, Image

New retail Managers don't know what they are doing. Usually they have been promoted as a matter of course from retail sales, where they have shown some aptitude, and it is assumed that they will transfer these skills to those they now supervise.

I didn't know anything about training, but I felt that as a student of the Art of Guiding, I might be able to pass along a few things I had noticed over the years. Maybe I could help them become at least Amateur Guides and together we could develop some Tours that were practical for our Jungle.

We began our first training the next Saturday morning, one hour before the store opened. Saturdays were the only day everyone worked, and since I closed, I made the sacrifice and came in on my time off. I laid down a few ground rules, the most important coming from the ***Lord of the Flies***, "you may not speak without the conch shell." The part of the conch was played by a small ruler known in the industry as a "P.D. Stick," so if you held the stick, you held the speaking floor.

After making certain everyone had coffee, a donut and a chance to use the restroom, we began.

"Welcome!" I hoped to make this light. "We need to make some improvement if our sales numb…."

The stick was snatched from my hand so fast that it almost made an audible snap.

"It's not us," Inez began.

Inez was interesting and important to the store success. The mall had a lot of Hispanic customers, and Inez spoke fluent Spanish. The problem was she spoke it on the phone for hours at a time during store hours. I had noticed this early on and made a comment about it after a ninety-minute conversation.

"It was a patient," she pointed out, quickly becoming defensive.

"Inez, I'm not fluent but I took conversational Spanish for two years. You were discussing a soap opera." I said.

She was careful with her correction. "Yeah, but I was discussing it with a patient."

Inez did possess the stick, so in accordance with the rule I listened.

"Anyways," she said, "it's not us. We all know what we are doing; there are just no customers."

The mall published figures each month from all the merchants and through some complex mathematical formula was able to give estimates of the number of people who visited the mall monthly. If we received a percent of a percent of the mall traffic in sales we would be too busy to be having these meetings. I pointed this out.

"Look, I'm not blaming anyone," I said as she handed back the ruler. "I'm just interested in how you view our situation."

Beside Inez was Kirk. He was a young upcoming superstar. He didn't know it yet, because the operative word in his description was "young." Once he gained a little experience he would develop quickly because he was a great listener and really wanted to be something in life. Like most young superstars, he just hadn't figured out what that something was.

The last person was Jackie. She was our *Office Mouse*. Office mice happily scurry around though the day quietly completing menial tasks which most workers tend to detest. She would make certain fresh coffee was always in the pot; check that the restroom was spotless and sufficiently stocked; and handle the mail, the deliveries, the inventory and the register reconciliation. Everything Jackie accepted as her direct responsibility was actually the responsibility of everyone in the store. If you noticed the restroom needed tending or an area needed vacuuming or dusting, you were supposed to jump in and take care of the task. But everyone knew if you waited five minutes Jackie would probably have it done for you, without even asking, and it would probably be done better than you would have done it yourself.

The problem was, I couldn't afford the luxury of an Office Mouse. I also couldn't afford a novice superstar, or a bilingual soap opera announcer. I needed four capable Sales Guides.

Faced with this situation my Regional Manager gave the customary response, "Let them go. You have the power to change employees and this is an "at will" State. If they aren't the right people, then let them go and find the right people."

"Wow!" I thought, as usual to myself. "That's a last resort."

There was no reason to let them go since each possessed some skills that were beneficial to the group. But I did need them focused and working together. It sounds corny, but I did need them to become a team, even if it was in spirit. If anyone wanted to leave, that would be up to them. However, I didn't have time for excuses when it came to improvement, so if there were issues they had with the business I needed to know those in advance.

"Let me put it simply." They were expecting the same "you need to do better" push they had received in the past. "Tell me in five words or less what's stopping us from doing more business."

Surprisingly, it was the Mouse who spoke up first, ruler forgotten.

"Our prices are too high," she said flatly. "Just the other day I tried to help a customer, but when I told her the price she said that was too much and then went to one of the other stores."

As I watched the others they all nodded. They all believed this was true.

"We take too long." It was Kirk. "I had someone come by this week who said he needed new glasses but he wanted them right away. He ended up going to another store because they could make them right away."

Again, they were all nodding.

"Inez? Anything?" I prodded her for a reason as I wanted them all committed to both this conversation about the problems, and the eventual solutions.

"I think we need lab coats," she said.

I didn't answer right away, but looked and saw them all nodding.

"Why do you think we need lab coats?" I asked, hoping that they would be able to come up with the last true issue I had been able to recognize before the meeting and had written in my notes.

"I think we lose a lot of patients to the new doctor's office at the end of the mall." She got it! Now I was hoping Inez would nail it down. "I spoke with one of our patients, the one I was on the phone with the other day when you told me to get off the phone."

(She had to say that. That was Inez. She was a terrier. Once she got hold of something she wanted to point out she wouldn't let it go until it was dead and flopping from her mouth.)

I smiled and waited for her to finish her thought.

Inez's glare faded. "Anyway she said that she was taking her grandmother there instead because her grandmother needed a more complicated prescription, and they seemed to know more. Well, I know a girl who works there and I know ten times more than she does about glasses and prescriptions."

I kept hoping for the words I wanted to hear. "Come on Inez," I silently rooted, "say it."

Inez came through. "I was just thinking that we're not representing ourselves as professionally as we could. And I thought, maybe, that lab coats would help."

Bingo! I could have kissed her.

OK, they did their part, now it was time for me to do mine as a manager and bring it all home. "I've been taking notes," I lied. I should have said I've *taken* notes, because my notes were the ones I had written before the meeting. I had hoped that my staff was smart enough to recognize the obvious problems, and interested enough in improvement to verbalize them. "Here are the three situations I need to help you on."

"Price objections." I pointed to Jackie who nodded vigorously.

"Customer service." Kirk was smiling and nodding.

"And store image." Inez nodded once in a definitively curt manner.

I looked at the books. Nobody was booked for the entire day until two-thirty. The only potential customers would be walk-ins, and I felt I could handle better walk-ins better than they now could, so I made an executive decision. I rewarded them for their input and time. The decision was made easier because I had already realized that whether or not they were present was having little impact on sales.

"You are all still on the clock." I pointed this out so they understood that, whatever I asked them to do, they were still getting paid. "Here are three movie passes for the theatre next door. The first showings start at nine-thirty. Here is a twenty for snacks. Go see a movie, eat lunch and be back here by one o'clock to finish your shifts."

They looked at me as though I was insane.

"You want us to go to a movie?"

"Yes."

"At ten o'clock in the morning, on a Saturday?"

"Yes," I answered.

"Which one?" they asked. The theatre was a multiplex so there were several to choose from.

"It doesn't matter to me." I said. "But you need to all agree on which movie and all see the same movie. Lunch has no rules, just all of you be back here by one o'clock."

They just stood there.

"Go!" I finally said, and they wandered out like children lost in a fog.

The store's weekly sales gross was usually around two thousand dollars. By the time they had returned there were seven new order trays sitting in the back and almost three thousand dollars in cash and checks in the register. The Mouse squeaked, the Superstar stood in awe, and the Announcer crossed herself and said "Dios mio."

I simply said, "Hey, I'm kind of hungry. I'm going to go to lunch. I'll be back in an hour or so. You three can handle the store while I'm out, right?"

They all just stood there, finally nodding slightly.

"Kirk," I said while leaving, "how was the movie?"

He was still glazed, it took a second. "Good," he finally said. "It was, ah, good."

"Cool!" I said and went to lunch.

CHAPTER EIGHTEEN
Improving Image

The week went pretty well. Sales happened and very little was said, but the fact that most of the sales happened while I was there by myself became obvious to everyone.

I wasn't surprised. Often allowing the spark of talent to bloom is like planting seeds in a garden. On the surface it can appear for weeks that nothing is happening, and then all of a sudden tiny plants are everywhere.

Potential Guides are like this as well. They need nurturing to sprout. Some, unfortunately, never make it. They are duds. And, sometimes you nurture someone only to discover what you thought was going to produce a pretty flower ends up turning into a weed.

Its par for the Retail Jungle and it doesn't matter.

Duds can be quickly identified by their lack of growth.

Weeds can be pulled.

As I said earlier, not everyone is cut out to be a Guide.

But by supporting the location through my own efforts, I was buying time for my staff to grow. By refraining from discussing anything about sales during the week, I was sending the message that I was comfortable that we had addressed the issues and we were proceeding to make corrections and adjustments appropriately. The staff needed to feel confident in me. It was that thought which made me realize the power of The Expert and understand that it was the first of the three areas I needed to tackle.

Saturday came, and once again we were all there at eight. That was a good sign in my book. Tardiness without good cause, while

I've never documented it, is probably one of the best indicators of work ethic for retail. It should be the first rule explained about any job and it is often overlooked. Here's an example:

"Welcome to Sammy's House of Pancakes," says Mr. Sam Carbonie to his new hire. "We have chosen you from the hundreds of minimum-wage candidates to be our *Good Morning Greeter*. You will stand by the reception desk and greet everyone with the phrase 'Welcome to Sammy's House of Pancakes! Home of the Endless-Stack™.'"

"Thank you Mr. Carbonie. I won't let you down," says the kid.

"Alright kid, here's your pancake costume, your pad-o-butter mittens and your syrup container hat. Make us proud."

The kid asks, "Mr. Carbonie, what's my schedule?"

"Six to noon," says the King of Cakes™.

The next morning the kid doesn't show up for work because his dog got sick. The following day he walks in at six-fifteen and says his alarm didn't go off, his bicycle broke and he didn't realize that if you put the mittens on first you can't zip up the pancake costume.

Carbonie loses it and fires the kid, rightfully so.

Do you know why?

Because the first rule of a job, any job, is to be there on time. The rest of the job requires some action that relies on skills and abilities you will need to exercise, but the first rule requires nothing more than moving from point "A" to point "B" and arriving on time. People do this for everything - movies, sporting events, dates, dinners, TV shows and doctor appointment - daily without any problems. It's even the first rule you learn as a child.

```
("Hey! I've got to go #2! I better start
heading towards the potty or I'm going to be late
and there will be ramifications!")
```

So my staff made it and I didn't have to deal with any of the ramifications of tardiness.

Over the next hour, I explained my theory on The Expert, and how each of them already was an expert in his or her own right. They each knew several key features of frames, lenses and contacts which they could use to enforce their expertise. After all, all you really need is one or two pertinent facts that the Tourist doesn't.

"The problem with each of you is the *Wizard of Oz* syndrome," I said.

They looked at me blankly.

"You know, like the movie?" I asked.

Not a word.

"The Wizard of Oz? Dorothy? The Lion? The Scarecrow?"

"What are you talking about?" asked Inez.

I was amazed. This has happened to me several times over the years and every time it happens I am knocked back on my heels. I understand it's possible that someone never heard an obscure song by some random band, or doesn't know the name or team stats of a specific sports figure, and it's even possible that some television shows have come and gone without much notice. But when it's something as iconic as *The Wizard of Oz*, you would expect everybody to know what you're talking about.

I dated a girl once who honestly had no idea what *The Beverly Hillbillies* was. She said that though she had grown up with a television in her home, she had never even *(accidentally)* happened upon the show and could not relate to any reference I made to it. We broke up several days later because every conversation we had from that point forward started with me saying, "Really? You **NEVER** heard of *The Beverly Hillbillies*?" It preyed on my mind and I couldn't let it drop. Finally, it got to be too much and we broke up. When she left, she yelled over her shoulder, "Why don't you go find Mary Lou Crumpet and date her!" As she drove off I was still yelling, "It's Elly May Clampett, and she at least would have admitted having seen the show!"

To save time I gave them a brief synopsis of the storyline. They sat rapt in attention. I even did my best to do some of the voices.

"So you're giving us a diploma?" asked Kirk when I finished the story.

"No. I don't have to," I said. "The whole point of the Wizard was to show them that they already had the abilities they sought;

they just needed to realize it for themselves and gain the confidence to use the skills they already possessed."

Jackie asked, "So you're giving us watches shaped like hearts?"

"No. I'm not giving you watches."

Inez spoke up, "Well then, what's the point of your story?"

At that point I walked to the closet and handed each person a crisp white lab coat. I had had their names embroidered on each coat with a title clearly imprinted under each. Jackie's boldly stated "Customer Excellence Advisor." Kirk's listed him as "Strategic Vision Consultant," and Inez' promoted her adeptness as "Optical Technology Liaison."

They took the jackets with reverence and it was the Mouse who asked, "What do these titles mean?"

I smiled. "They mean whatever you want them to mean, Jackie. But, like the Wizard, let me tell you all this. There are people who work with customers daily. They help them find what they need to make their lives better, and they have no more skills than all of you, but what they do have is a title. So, by the power invested in me as General Manager I now pronounce you Experts Emeritus in the Fraternity of the Retail Guides, and I empower you with the ability to help without fear everyone who walks into our shop. You are hereby granted the opportunity to be the finest representative you can be."

Kirk asked the right question. "But what does a Customer Excellence Advisor, a Strategic Vision Consultant or an Optical Technology Liaison do?"

"They do whatever you think they should do," I said. "I took away the mold, now it's up to you." They needed to mull this over and think about it. "Here's some money and some movie passes. You know the drill. Be back by one o'clock."

Lesson #20 – Every Professional Guide understands: the only limits to being a better Guide are those you set on yourself. You are empowered and you have the authority, the ability and the right to be the best at any job you undertake.

The changes began that weekend. Another impressive morning would have been enough, but it was the surprise of several sales made during my absence that made my day. Three more trays with some impressive high-end frames sat in the order area. As I reviewed the orders, I noticed they were all for a single customer, yet each was signed as sold by a different employee. I didn't ask, they told me.

"You won't believe this!" Jackie was bouncing off the floor with excitement. "This guy came in to buy a pair of glasses and I said 'Hi, how may I help you?'"

Inez cut her off, "So Jackie starts helping him and says 'Let's ask our Optical Technology Liaison which lenses you should use.'"

Kirk started talking over the other two, "So I went over and explained about our sunglass promotion and told him that my job as Strategic Vision Consultant was to be sure all his vision needs were met."

"And I told him," Jackie squeaked up, "that my job as Customer Excellence Advisor was to make certain his experience with our office was better than in any place he had ever purchased eyewear before."

Inez didn't want to be outdone. "And I explained that as Optical Technology Liaison, I was making certain that all suggestions were correct and in the best interest of his vision, eye protection and long term satisfaction."

I was smiling. "Where did you get those job descriptions?"

"I don't know," said Kirk. "We just kind of made them up over lunch. Are they OK?"

There was just one clarification I needed. "Do you feel they are helpful to the customers? Do they allow you to do your job and be the best you can be?" They all nodded.

"Yeah," I smiled. "I think they're great!"

"There was only one problem," said Inez. "We had another customer that had a prescription and was going to buy two pairs, but when we told her it was going to take a week to get her glasses she said she was going to go to that store that does the glasses same-day."

"For now," I started "forget it. You all are doing great. Maybe we should handle that topic next weekend."

"Customer service?" asked Kirk.

"Yes, sir!" I said.

Over the next six days I began to see a change in my staff. Shoes were shined; the general dress was a little better. Jackie and Inez began to use a little make-up, something I know shouldn't make any difference in a person's skills but which showed a general trend toward confidence and a reflection on their representation of self to the customers. Kirk even began wearing tie - although they were all raucous disasters. It didn't matter. Kirk was trying to be a Strategic Vision Consultant and he had decided at some point that S.V.Cs wore wild-colored ties. I asked him about it when we had a minute.

"It's alright, isn't it?" Kirk asked.

I bit my lip. "Yeah, Kirk, it's fine. It sure is, um, colorful." Today's mix was neon blue with fat yellow dots.

He blushed. "Yeah. I know. But let me show you something." He took me to the order area and started going through his orders for the week. "Do you remember Monday when I wore that red tie?"

How could I forget? The tie had huge red walruses frolicking in navy blue waters.

"Well, look," he said, while handing me an order tray. It wasn't clear to me what I was supposed to be looking for until he made it clear. "When was the last time we sold a red frame?"

He was right. I couldn't recall us selling something this colorful in quite some time; the fashion then was grey or brown eyewear.

"On Tuesday I had that one with the balloons." He meant the one with green hot air balloons flying in an orange sunset. Tuesday he had sold two pairs of glasses. Both had green frames.

"I think I'm on to something," Kirk said. "Maybe when people see me wearing these colors it sort of empowers them to be a little bold in their color choices, or maybe in a subliminal way I'm influencing their decisions."

I asked the only question I could think of at the moment. "Are the customers happy with what you're suggesting?"

Kirk beamed. "Yeah! They love it! But I don't want to stop there. I think a part of being a Strategic Vision Consultant may be helping customers understand that colors can affect more than just a person's outward look. They can set a tone to your appearance."

"I think you're on to something, Kirk. How would you like to take over next week's meeting and explain your idea to the group?"

"Me?" he was shocked.

"Well, you've explained a concept to me that I've never heard. On this subject you're now the Expert. Do you think you can explain it to everyone?" I hoped he could.

"Yes, sir." Kirk was becoming a Professional Color Guide and probably didn't even know it. "Yes, sir, I'd be happy to do that."

Saturday came, Kirk did great, and the next week Inez and Jackie started wearing colorful scarves with their clean pressed lab coats. The colors changed daily, sometimes two or three times during the same day. I would hear weird things coming from them like, "I'm just not feeling purple right now. I'm way more fuchsia." This was usually followed by "Do we have any fuchsia frames on the boards?"

The following Wednesday the three came to me with a demand.

"Can you please get with the program? We're sick of that black tie you wear every day, it's depressing."

Lesson #21 – A Professional Guide "gets with the program."

Sales were beginning to happen fairly regularly, but the store was still way below where we needed it to be on the P&L statement. I needed to get the staff more money, more help and more respect from the District Office. All of that was possible through only one direction - more sales.

We needed to address the second issue, Customer Service.

CHAPTER NINETEEN
Service: Rules of the Tour

The Saturday morning meeting of the Fraternity of Retail Guides was called to order. Kirk had brought a large thermos of coffee and the best damn crumb-cake I had ever tasted.

"It's from my Mom," he admitted. "I had to stop there this morning to bring my Dad back his toenail clippers."

(The three of us all looked at each other and you could tell we had the same thought, "Geez, you borrow your parents' toenail clippers? Yuck!" but nobody said it. Still, we should have checked with each other before Christmas shopping that year. Poor Kirk opened three gifts at our party, all identical toenail clippers. That was embarrassing.)

With the holiday clipper incident still months in the future, Kirk continued. "And my Mom had baked this for me because she knows how much I like it."

He had every reason to like it; as far as breakfast pastry goes this was fantastic.

"Kirk," I asked, "did she make it for you this morning?"

Kirk swallowed some cake. "Yeah. She bakes almost every morning."

"We've got to have this recipe," Jackie and Inez said in unison.

"You can't," Kirk explained. "She won't give it out. She says it was her great-great grandmother's recipe and it can only be passed down from mother to daughter."

Inez was breaking hers apart while she ate it. "What the heck is in this? Is that celery? Celery and strawberries?"

"I think its rhubarb."

We all kept eating, and for a flickering moment we all disliked Kirk for his stupid Y chromosome, which appeared to have thwarted our immediate access to the divine secrets of heavenly crumb-cakeness. We all, of course, immediately forgave him on the next bite, and hoped he would soon find a nice girl to settle down with and produce a crumb-cake-recipe-acceptable daughter.

"Wow. This is unbelievable!" I took another piece. "She bakes this every day?" I was in awe.

"No, only on Saturdays." Kirk filled us in on his mother's baking schedule. "On Sundays she bakes bread because bread takes a long time to make. Some days it's cookies; some days she makes rolls. She only makes crumb-cake on Saturdays."

Inez asked, "What if you want crumb-cake on a Wednesday?"

"Too bad, he said. "You just have to wait."

The light bulb came on in my head. "Is this worth the wait?"

Three faces, like children, with cinnamon crumbles around the corners of the mouths looked at me and silently asked "You're kidding, right?"

"Guys," I knew they would understand it now, "that's the secret of customer service."

They call it a "flash of genius," that moment when an inventor realizes the secret to developing a device which changes the world from that moment forward. People generally refer to it as the moment "the light bulb came on." We all referred to it as "crumb-cake awareness" because we all knew it was that breakfast food that changed our world from that moment forward.

Kirk's mother proved to us that you can set boundaries and still satisfy completely. Customer service didn't revolve around the rules we all had had drilled into our heads for years like "under-promise and over-deliver" or "the customer always comes first." These are vague dogmas from people who are trying to politely say, "I have no actual advice, but you're not doing well enough and you need to do better." They are as silly as telling someone "You need to give a hundred-and-ten percent," which is by definition impossible.

At that moment we all understood the key features of customer service, if only in a crumb-cakey vague sort of way.

1. The baker sets the rules.

Kirk's mom had other things to do during the week, and Kirk understood that. The bread she baked made sandwiches for everyone's lunches throughout the week. Kirk demanding crumb-cake on Sundays would have been unfair and disruptive. His Mother didn't argue the point with Kirk; she simply stated the fact that no crumb-cake was available on any day but Saturday.

2. The Baker fills the order exactly as expected.

Every Saturday, Kirk's mom did what she promised. She made this divine ambrosia. She didn't make eggs, bacon, pancakes or waffles. She didn't make cinnamon rolls, Danish, cupcakes or brownies. She made crumb-cake. It was exactly what Kirk wanted and it was exactly what he received.

3. Absolutely perfect crumb-cake retains customers.

Maintaining a high standard for products and services is key. This rule means a lot when it comes to bakery.

My own mother was a fantastic cook as well. She enjoyed making cookies, and though she never quite got the recipe for Grandma's molasses cookies down, she made some fantastic cookies of her own like chocolate chip, peanut-butter, almond fingers, thumbprints and on and on.

Over the years I have lost my sweet-tooth, and my sister has taken over as the family matriarch, handling most of the cooking and holiday meals. My Mother, well into her eighties, has simplified her retirement cooking to soup, sandwiches and simple dinners which keep her and my father fed and content.

Last summer, during our annual family retreat, Mother was going through post-post-post partum depression and got a bee in her bonnet that baking me cookies for my birthday would send these feelings back into remission for another forty years, or at least long enough for her to find a comfortable resting spot for herself, her favorite dress and a pine box. Knowing the effort it was going to take, I asked that she refrain from her endeavor and just slip me five bucks in a card, but she persisted.

"Come on, honey," she said holding my hand in both of hers, "let me do this for you. I'll make you whatever kind of cookies you want. What kind should I make you?"

I figured I had one last chance to allow her a gracious out on a technicality. Over the years time has taken a toll on my mother's hands. You can feel it in their fragility. The skin has grown thin and a slight amount of arthritis has set in; her muscles tend to shake with the unsteadiness of the elderly. All of this makes this dear, sweet, gentle woman unlikely to pursue a task that demanded intensive hand labor.

I looked upon the soft eyes of the woman who bore me, nurtured me and raised me and played my last card.

"Pinwheel cookies," I said.

"Are you f**king crazy?" said my eighty-seven year old Mother.

"Mom!" I was shocked.

"Do you know how much work pinwheel cookies are?" She was clearly upset. "I'm not making you those."

"Good." Problem solved.

She looked at me, her eyes narrowing. Mothers can always read their children. Maybe it's a maternal link, or maybe it's because they have known your feeble attempts at skirting the truth all your life. In any event, Mother read me like a book and knew I was trying to buffalo her.

"No, no, no," she came back, "you want pinwheel cookies; I'm making you pinwheel cookies."

"Honest, Mom, you really don't have to." Too late. I had ticked her off and now it was personal.

For the uninformed, let me describe. Pinwheel cookies are chocolate and vanilla sugar cookies without icing. As cookies go, they are pretty easy to make.

There's really nothing too difficult about making cookies. You just follow the recipe, mix the ingredients (milk, eggs, butter, sugar, flour and baking soda), bake as needed and presto - you have cookies.

Pinwheel cookies get their name from the handwork required to shape the dough into the pinwheels. The dough needs to be made, and then divided into two batches: one with extra sugar and cocoa and one with extra sugar and vanilla. The dough is then chilled, and once cool, rolled out very thin. The two sheets are stacked, then curled together, forming a tube. The cookies are produced by slicing the tube sideways to show the spirals of chocolate and vanilla cookie dough. These are, for me, heaven.

The next day Mother arrived at the house with a box. Inside the box were four dozen perfect pinwheel cookies.

"Thanks, Mom," I said, and I meant it.

"It was no problem, honey," she said.

At that point the kids showed up.

"What are these?" the kids asked.

"Pinwheel cookies," I said. "Grandma made them for my birthday."

"Can we have some?"

"Sure," I said.

My nephew and niece were there along with my stepchildren, so we left for the family room with cold milk in hand to enjoy the bounty while my parents sat in the kitchen with a coffee to attack the newspaper's crossword puzzle.

I told them about pinwheel cookies, and how they were one of my favorites when I was a kid. I explained the work that went into these and we actually talked about what a "labor of love" is. Finally, I divided the cookies up, saving a few for my sister and her husband, and we all took a bite.

"These are awful," my nephew said, emptying the chewed cookie into his hand. The bland floury taste was apparent to everyone who had a cookie in his mouth.

My stepchildren looked at me, gagging, "These are your favorite cookies?"

Milk was downed at a great rate as we all attempted to wash the dead taste from our mouths. Obviously something was wrong. The children all got the giggles and my niece was first to state the obvious, "I think Grandma forgot something in the recipe."

It was the sugar.

It doesn't hurt my memories of those cookies; in fact it makes this particular one more memorable. It caused a lot of laughing, especially for my father, who had snuck one fresh off the rack from the oven and didn't have the decency to tell us all what was in store. He even explained that he saw the un-added sugar sitting in the measuring cup right on the dryer during the mixing and didn't see the need to point it out. Mother had apparently gotten distracted while doing laundry, and not finding the sugar which she knew she had measured out, simply assumed she had added it already and proceeded with the recipe.

The only residual effect is, I'll never ask Mother for pinwheel cookies again.

But if we take the pinwheels as an example and the crumb-cake as another example, then the message becomes clear. You'll jump through hoops to get something you think is wonderful and you'll return, again and again, until something happens to change the circumstance.

Inez expressed what we were all feeling. "We need to create a better crumb-cake recipe," meaning our Tour. "Ours isn't that good."

Kirk added to the discussion. "If we make the experience good enough, then the customers might not mind waiting for their glasses, like I don't mind waiting for the cake."

Jackie finished the thought, "We might stop losing so many customers to the competition, too. But what about attracting new ones?"

Kirk had it, but he looked to me for confirmation, "Word of mouth?"

I agreed. It made perfect sense. If you do something right, you don't need to waste much time or money attracting customers. They tend to find you and tell others.

Inez wanted to be clear. "But this isn't crumb-cake, its eyeglasses."

"What's the difference?" I asked.

Lesson #22 – Sell balloons or bakery, sell eyeglasses or slippers, sell jewelry or underwear; the situation never changes because the three key retail components are always present; Guide, Tourist and Tour.

So we set about improving our recipe. Building a better crumb-cake is a book in and of itself. (Do we hear sequel?)

But let me give you a brief outline of the process of improving sales through improving your Tour:

1. You <u>can't</u> change the basic ingredients.

So if you work in a store that sells sweaters, you can't start selling suits as a way to be a better sweater store. You need to work within the confines of what's available. If you're selling sweaters, and want to improve, you need to build a better Sweater Tour.

2. But, you usually <u>can</u> control the *quality* of the ingredients.

No problem selling mylar balloons in a balloon store, they're more colorful and they last longer.

3. And, you <u>can</u> change the associated service, but only procedures you can *directly* control.

Suppose you sell custom draperies. You can shorten the amount of time it takes to set an appointment and you can be on time for every appointment you make, but you might not be able to control manufacturing time once you send the order to the factory, so don't even attempt it. Any retail that demands a form of product customization or special ordering takes the exact time of delivery out of the Guide's hands.

Time, in most cases, is actually no big problem.

Imagine you want to take a vacation. Very few people can leave immediately, even if they have the funds available. Preparation time is part of life. For a trip, it takes time to decide where you'd like to go, research travel arrangements, make reservations and so on. The amount of time something takes is actually less important than just meeting the expected time of delivery.

The important part of scheduling delivery in a Retail Jungle is to be aware of the current flow, and master what you can personally control.

4. Finally, you need to constantly monitor your position.

Every type of guide uses a map and a compass. You need to find yours and refer to it constantly. If you want to create a new path through the Jungle, you need to know two important specific points: where you are and where you want to go. A compass is just a reference tool you use to check your bearing between those two points.

In sales, your reference tool only works when you have a sincere desire to improve, coupled with the ability to look objectively at your current situation. Those are your bearing points: where you want to be, and, realistically, where you are now. If you ever feel you're lost along the way, you need to trust your gut instincts. If you're still in doubt, your progress is easily verifiable by the amount of money in the cash drawer at the end of a day.

A smart person references change in everything, even baking. Changing a crumb-cake recipe by adding more cinnamon may seem to be a great idea, or it could throw the balance of flavors completely askew. So you add a little more, bake one, and then monitor the change by tasting the result. If it's better, great; and if it's not better, look for improvement elsewhere.

Inez had taken the lead on our technology. She felt it was her duty since she had been empowered to lead us in that area. Within two weeks, manufacturer's representatives were showing up and sending us information on advances and new lenses, and we began revamping our suggested offerings.

Kirk finished reading up on color, becoming quite an expert, and moved his focus to shape and style. Frame reps from manufacturers were sending us samples to review and offering their information on current style trends around the globe. Our inventory began to change.

Jackie - now more a lion than a mouse - began to look at our process for sales and chart how we handled customers at every point. More than anyone else, she believed in the compass theory. And, while she trusted her internal compass, she wanted absolute proof; so she recorded everything we did. This turned out to be an extremely important step which made a tremendously positive difference to our improvement plan.

Lesson #23 – *You cannot understand where you need to improve a Tour until you completely understand exactly what it is you're currently doing and have a handle on where you're currently leading Tourists.*

Jackie wanted us all to be excellent. As the Excellence Advisor she wanted to have a major role in helping to revamp our Tour, but she wanted us all to understand exactly what it was we were currently doing, along with "where and why" we made every change in hopes of improvement.

It worked.

We all learned. Once we examined the process as a group we found out nobody had the real answer, but we all had our strengths and weaknesses. I got shot down just as much as everybody else once we examined all her notes. As a scribe, the Mouse/Lion was brutally honest and only Inez ever argued with her observations.

Just once.

"Are you calling me a liar?" Jackie was standing over Inez with a look of fire in her eyes. I tried to calm down the situation.

"Hey, hey, hey now," I jumped in. "Maybe you didn't get all the details." I tried to feather out her anger by helping her to be retrospective.

"I think you're over-reacting," said Inez.

Jackie regained a little composure but restated the facts.

"Inez," she said, "you were in charge of Mr. Munoz' order, correct?"

"Yes," said Inez. This was beginning to look like a trial and Jackie had all the fervor of a prosecuting attorney making a case.

"And on May 19th, you were assigned the task of contacting the manufacturing laboratory to verify that the order was proceeding as planned, correct?" Jackie continued.

"Well, yes, but…"

Jackie cut her off. "And if there was any delay, you were to contact Mr. Munoz to let him know. Is that correct?"

This was better than a TV show. Inez was starting to sweat.

"Well, yeah. But…" Again she was cut off.

"You didn't. You didn't call and now Mr. Munoz won't have his glasses in time for his vacation." Jackie was still standing. I was waiting for the verdict.

Jackie turned to me as if I was a judge or jury.

"Fire her," said Jackie.

I was so shocked I almost spit out my crumb-cake. (Almost)

"Jackie," I said, "I know we all agreed on the Rules of the Tour, but hang on."

The Rules of the Tour was an eight-page agreement, signed by all of us a few weeks earlier detailing the exact way to handle customers and orders. It was our new and improved crumb-cake recipe and it was a doozey. It had taken months to collect the data and weeks to analyze the system looking for flaws or places to improve. As in developing a new recipe, we had gone through a lot of flops and mistakes. We learned that making small changes in one area could have dramatic repercussions in another, but over time the Rules of the Tour blossomed into a work of perfection. Jackie's work of perfection to be exact, because, like Thomas Jefferson, she had drafted the rules herself and then demanded we all sign an oath of fealty to them. They were posted in our "sanctum-sanctorum" (restroom) where we could spend every seated moment reviewing the document and our signatures agreeing to live by these rules each and every day. She had taken the role of Customer Excellence Advisor to new heights of seriousity.

I spoke to Kirk, who appeared to be the bailiff in this trial. "Buddy, what's your view on this?"

Kirk turned it back on me. "Would you still like the crumb-cake if my mom forgot the nutmeg?"

At this point the court took an emergency three-minute recess as some of us said they needed time for the restroom. Actually, nobody went to the restroom; we all snuck off to different corners of the office and added nutmeg to the secret lists we kept to try to decipher Kirk's mother's crumb-cake recipe.

"Nutmeg," I thought while scribbling, "how could I have not guessed nutmeg? I love nutmeg!"

When we all returned, I continued. "No, Kirk, you're right. It wouldn't be the same without nutmeg." Eyes darted back and forth, "But I might still enjoy it if she omitted the cardamom."

"There's no cardamom in it, I think," said Kirk and you could see us all mentally scratching that one off our lists.

Kirk's eyes were daggers when he realized I had detoured the conversation, so I retraced my steps, knowing I should get back to the point and stop attempting to uncover more of the secret recipe.

"You're right, Kirk, it wouldn't be the same." I admitted.

Inez realized then that her days of excuses were over. She had signed the Rules of the Tour as we all did. Not because it was required, but because by that point we were all truly committed to improvement. We had evolved into a team. The movie days and the lunches were a part of it, but the bigger part hinged on the reality that for the past few months now, we all had a common goal. We weren't trying to deliver a-hundred-and-ten percent, but we were through delivering seventy-five percent.

Luckily, two of the tour rules saved Inez from immediate dismissal - probably the two best rules Jackie had incorporated into the entire Rules of the Tour.

- **Never lie.** To clients or customers, staff or supervisors, manufacturers or vendors or anyone we do business with in any way or on any level.
- Understand always that <u>we are not perfect, and neither are the customers</u>. Give leniency where you can, make improvements where you may, and correct that which can be corrected efficiently, effectively and to the very best of your ability. Also accept that there will be things you cannot correct, and have the wisdom to accept this, and to know the difference.

That second one was written by Jackie without any input from anyone else, and it prompted us all to speculate that the Mouse, although never bringing it up in the office, was in all likelihood either a devout Catholic or a recovering alcoholic. Either way, she understood and appreciated redemption and forgiveness.

Inez lost all harshness from her voice and spoke to Jackie and Kirk in a tone of true humility and repentance. "Look," she said, "I'm sorry. I didn't call the lab and the order is going to arrive a day later than we planned. It was my fault. Mr. Munoz won't have time to pick them up here but I think we can get them to him before his vacation."

"How?" I asked.

"It's my responsibility, leave it to me," Inez said.

The phone call came to me at seven-fifty-one in the morning. I took it only because I was asleep and my arm acted on its own accord without regard to my brain.

"Hey, Boss, did I catch you at a bad time?"

"It's seven-fifty-one, Inez. There is no 'good time' for me before eight." I heard the noise in the background. "Where are you?"

"I'm at the airport. I just got through fitting Mr. Munoz' glasses and I'm going to be heading back to the office, but with morning traffic I might be a little late. I wanted you to know in advance."

This was our policy, to call in before you're late. Her mission just hit home. "Inez, how did you get Mr. Munoz' glasses? The delivery courier doesn't come in until almost ten."

"I know," she said. "I drove to the courier's sort site and intercepted the delivery truck at six o'clock. Then I hightailed it over to the airport to fit the glasses on Mr. Munoz before his flight."

My head was spinning. "How did you know his flight?"

The next five minutes involved a convoluted story about Mr. Munoz telling Inez about his vacation because he and his wife were going to the same hotel featured on the Spanish soap opera Inez watches, Inez' cousin who works for the airlines, calls to family members and the avoidance of a minor car accident. I just listened in amazement.

"So can you cover for me if I'm ten minutes late?"

Managers can be so very mean sometimes, when it's so simple to be so very nice.

Nice *IS* simple.

"Certainly," I told her. "Drive safe and take your time."

CHAPTER TWENTY
Everyone on Board?

It wasn't all written down. Some of the improvements were so simple and clever that we just found them and did them without looking back.

Every Jungle has its quiet times, and today was ours. The mall itself was deserted, probably due to the torrential rains.

It had been over a year since my own last eye exam, so when I spoke with the doctor and found that they had a family of five cancel, I asked if she wouldn't mind checking me out. She agreed, and told me to come by when I had a free hour.

Kirk arrived at ten, and I headed next door. It was a small, but typical, doctor's office. Angeline, the receptionist, was sitting behind the desk in her usual spot while the doctor was taking care of some business in her back office. She told me it would be a few minutes and motioned for me to have a seat.

Unlike our side, the doctor's office had been professionally redecorated. It had six chairs and a coffee table.

"This is a nice waiting room, Angeline." I spotted the magazine rack and got up. "What do people usually do while they're waiting, read?"

"It's not a 'waiting room,'" she corrected, "It's a 'reception area.'"

"OK. Then what do people usually do while they are 'recepting?'"

She missed the joke. I honestly think about ninety percent of all ironic humor is wasted.

"They read." And her head went back down to a book she had obviously brought in to entertain herself on slower days.

As I scanned the offerings in the magazine rack I understood why. A few issues of *Lowlights*© kids magazine, a worn out copy of *Sports Affinity*© and two *Better Bungalow*© issues that epitomized the term "dog-eared" were all that was available. Each issue was over three years old.

There was an idea here, but I didn't know how to capitalize on it. I had my eyes examined and returned to our shop. Inez and Jackie were reading something at the front desk. When I asked them what it was they held up a magazine and turned on the light bulb in my head.

"This is how Jackie wants to get her hair cut." Inez pointed to a picture, then flipped through a few pages. "But I told her this would look much better because of the shape of her face."

I turned on my heels and started walking out the door.

"Are you still on break?" Jackie asked as I was leaving.

"Not really."

I walked to the bookstore in the mall and looked at the magazine rack. Funny, it catches you by surprise sometimes, but there are about a thousand magazines published every month. I knew what I was looking for and started pulling copies down and making a pile. Ten came to just under fifty dollars, the maximum I was allowed to spend from petty cash without getting pre-authorization from my District Manager. Paid, packed and pumped I headed back to the shop.

"That was quick." Inez eyed the bag. "What did you get?"

"Tools." I said.

Jackie said that they looked more like magazines. I handed her the receipt for petty cash and told her to write on the receipt exactly what I said "sales tools."

"How are magazines sales tools?" asked Inez as she worked through the stack. *BQ*©, *Man's Wealth*©, *Cigar Enjoyerino*©, *Meg-um*© and *Sports Animated*© were in the men's pile.

"These are great," said Jackie, as she went though the women's magazines: *Emme*©, *Vague*© and *Fashion Daily*©, along with *Hollywood Update*© and *Eighteen*©.

"Are we supposed to read these?" Inez was already buried in the new copy of *Hollywood Update*©.

156

"No," I pulled out a pad of Paste-Its©. "They're for the doctor's office, but we're going to fix them before we drop them off."

Over the next hour we went through every page looking for anything pictured that was eye related. A picture of someone in glasses or sunglasses was obvious. If we recognized the product we noted the reference information on the back of a Paste-It and tagged the page so the note stuck out like a file marker. On the front of the note we wrote something suggestive:

Do you like the sunglasses Mario Lanza is wearing? They are available right next door!

But as we started looking at more and more pictures, the concept blossomed.

Inez found a head shot of a current actress for a cosmetics line and wrote:

Her eyes are blue. We can make your eyes the same color. Just stop next door.

This one referred to a line of eye-color-changing tinted contact lenses that we just released.

Jackie placed one on an advertisement for a *Grey&Darker©* belt sander that didn't even have a picture of a person in it:

Safety eyewear is the most important tool! Ten percent off all safety eyewear right next door.

By the time we finished, each magazine had a fringe of dozens of tags. Inez actually stuck my favorite on an ad for *RangeTop Stuffing©*:

Are your eyes as dry as bad turkey? See us next door for eye drops!

At the doctor's office, I began pulling all the old magazines. Angeline watched me with a suspicious eye and couldn't resist a comment.

"What do you think you're doing?"

"Updating your magazines," I said.

She watched me pick up the old magazines. "Those are the doctor's."

"These are the janitor's," I corrected.

The next day, Kirk and I were opening a shipment when a customer walked in with a magazine.

"Do you have these?" He was holding a prescription in one hand and a copy of *Sports Animated©* in the other. The magazine was open to a resort shot of a bikini-clad woman on a beach in Mexico.

"Women in bikinis?" Kirk asked.

I started laughing. I had forgotten to tell Kirk about the new sales tools and how they were supposed to work.

The girl in the picture was wearing a set of expensive designer sunglasses. We found out that his girlfriend wanted a pair just like them for an upcoming vacation.

"Did you need them in prescription?"

"No, she doesn't need glasses." Then he looked around. "But I guess I do. Can you show me something cool?"

Kirk had been paging through the magazine and now held it open to a Paste-It page showing a well-known musician in fashionable eyewear.

"Cool enough for him should be cool enough for you," said Kirk, picking up immediately on the concept, and off he went giving a Style Tour of the latest frames.

Over the next two weeks, the magazines appeared daily. The investment of about fifty dollars resulted in at least twenty sales we might never have received without our new sales tools.

Jackie the Mouse/Lion/Compass brought to our attention the only apparent flaw. We had received referrals from every magazine, except *Hollywood Update©*. The next time I stopped in the doctor's office, I looked for the magazine. There it sat in the rack, without any of the Paste-Its previously affixed.

"Angeline," I asked as she looked up from her book, "did you see a bunch of Paste-Its fall out of this magazine?"

She gave an exasperated sigh. "I took them out. They were bothering me when I was reading so I took them out of that one and threw them away. You should do that with all of them; those little tags get in my way."

Lesson #24 – *The fastest way to have a good Tour derailed is to forget outside influences. Always make certain everyone involved understands the "what" and "why."*

CHAPTER TWENTY-ONE
Price or Value

Despite Angeline's assistance, sales rose for almost a month straight, and then took a dramatic nose dive as we entered the home stretch before performance reviews. We needed to sharply re-evaluate.

"What's the number?" I asked, crumb-cake finished and coffee almost ready for a refill.

"About forty percent," Jackie seemed certain, then recanted. "Actually forty-two percent down these past two weeks." She wanted to be accurate. "'It' was better before they ran 'it', but 'it' looks bad."

By this point we had beaten most every other problem and were outselling two of our competitors. Our customer service had improved as we had found the sales path through our own Jungle that Tourists seemed to enjoy. We stopped shooting for unobtainable goals and simply concentrated on being as close to one-hundred percent as possible with every order. We didn't need to be amazing, just good, practical and consistent. Word got around; we were a business that people trusted.

Our image had changed. And, like the plot of the Lion, the Scarecrow and the Tin-Man, it was less about a little paint, some jackets and a few titles than it was about confidence, empowerment and attitude.

Sure, we still lost the occasional customer to the quick service store; we sent them business when our own customers needed something in a pinch. We had learned that everything doesn't go

The Retail Jungle

into the World's Best Crumb-cake, and that trying to be best at everything, doesn't make anything the World's Best.

We were more professional, but like just like image, it was less about our surface characteristics than something deeper. We had become a team: the Fraternity of the Retail Guides. That we had increased our knowledge of products and honed our procedures was wonderful, but the true benefit to our customers was that each and every one of us had become dedicated to being a Professional Guide, serving the Tourists, and giving them the Tour.

Yet, the numbers don't lie, and we were being affected by "it."

```
The "it" we were referring to was the recent
sale at the heavy discount competitor's location.
"It" was being advertised everywhere; on
television, in the newspapers, on the radio and,
most unfortunately, even on the kiosk almost
directly in front of our store. Since "it"
started, we had been losing sales and "it" was
definitely affecting the bottom line.
```

The worst part was that, although we understood exactly why this was happening, no one saw an easy way out.

"Can we match their deals? The only reason the customers appear to be leaving is price."

Kirk had asked a viable question, but he already knew the answer. While we had certain leeway for special package discounts and a few discretionary ones, `(such as ten percent off for seniors)`, our prices were set by our corporate offices.

I needed more information, so I turned to "La Brújula," as Jackie was affectionately dubbed by Inez, for a reading.

"Jackie, are they at least stopping in? How is our foot traffic? Are we certain price is the only reason?"

She paged through her log books.

"Yeah," and pages flipped, "from my count almost every patient at least stops in before going over there, and," she flipped again, "we're still getting a decent amount of walk-in shoppers, but we're climbing toward half of the customers we see asking our prices then leaving without making a purchase."

"Wow." `(I was back to "wow.")`

Jackie looked at her pages, then at me, then back to her pages. "Except for yours," she said after a second.

I had the last piece of crumb-cake half way to my mouth when her announcement caused every eye to turn to me, my hand, and the last piece of heaven for the week about to be a memory.

"What?" I asked, feeling embarrassed, but knowing in my heart that someone had to eat the last piece of heaven and this time it might as well be me.

"Your numbers are only down about five percent."

"And?" The cake disappeared in two quick bites. Actually my numbers weren't down at all; I had two sales the night before that hadn't yet registered. I was up for the week.

They all looked at me, and I knew why, and I knew what they expected of me, and by now, dear reader, you know I love this part.

So I paused...

And I waited a beat...

And I took a breath...

And I began the last Training Tour I ever did for the Fraternity of Retail Guides.

"It's time to talk about overcoming price objections," I said, and reached over to grab a bottle of water that Jackie had brought with her for the meeting.

Inez and I liked coffee, and although he hated it, Kirk dutifully poured himself a cup at every meeting simply because he wanted to look grown up, but Jackie always drank bottled water.

"Is everybody familiar with this?" I held up the bottle.

They looked at me as if I was joking.

"Water?" asked Kirk.

"No. *Bottled* water." I clarified, and heads nodded.

I went on, "Ok, you're all familiar with it and from time to time you've all bought this, right?" Again, heads nodded.

"Now think about this scene. You're in the middle of the Sahara desert and you're stranded. You walk over hills for days with no water anywhere to be found and you come upon a group of palm trees."

"Like an oasis?" Kirk asked.

"Right. Only there's no pond or well here. Instead there's a vending machine that has these pint-sized bottles of water for sale for ten dollars. You feel in your pocket and find a crumpled ten dollar bill…"

"Wouldn't it be dinars or shekels?" asked Inez.

"What?" she had broken my train of thought.

"Wouldn't it be ten **dinars** for the drink? Or whatever ten dollars US translates to in dinars? I mean it's in Africa, so the…"

"Inez, just go with me on this one, ok?" She quieted down.

"I think it's Krugerrands, isn't it?" Kirk knew I was trying to make a point here, but lately had found great pleasure in yanking my chain when he could.

Even Jackie got in on it. "No way. Ten Krugerrands is around five thousand dollars. Why would someone with five thousand dollars be stranded in the desert?"

They saw me prepare to argue the point, but then I realized that they were all smirking. "Fraternity" was a good description for our group; we had bonded, and hazing was an acceptable practice. Joke over, they motioned for me to go on. The mood was lighter now, and they were ready to learn.

"Tell us about the water, Boss."

Over the next hour I described perceived value. I had made my point that they would each gladly pay ten dollars for a bottle of water in the desert. Thirst, or the necessity of having something to drink in order to live, is an obvious reason for purchasing water. It was common sense. When I asked if they would make the purchase, everyone agreed they would. They had no choice. The water was an immediate required necessity; the perceived value of life, especially your own, is very high.

Next I described a scene where they were walking through a forest and came upon a pure mountain spring. Again, you are really thirsty, but in this instance fresh, clear, clean water was bubbling up right from the rocks. Next to the spring was the same vending machine with the same ten dollar price for bottled water. Nobody felt the need to make the purchase if the spring water was actually drinkable.

"Why waste the money?" was Jackie's response, which summed up everyone's feelings. I agreed and we made a mental note that competitive availability greatly influenced perceived value.

Finally we looked at our actual situation. Each of us agreed that from time to time we had each purchased bottled water; we agreed it was because we were thirsty, a basic need that required satisfying, but nobody was stranded in the desert, so we knew the purchases weren't driven by an immediate required necessity. Further, we all had homes with running water and even our tiny shop had a restroom sink where tap water could be had anytime.

So why were any of us ever purchasing bottled water?

They sat thinking about this for maybe three seconds when Inez opened the floor.

"It tastes better. The water here tastes funky."

I wrote "TASTE" on my note pad, then asked, "What else?" The answers started coming in rapid succession: convenience, choice of bubbled or flavored, even safety.

"What do you mean 'safety,' Jackie?" I asked.

It turns out that Jackie lived in a part of town that still used well water, and occasionally the wells would get a "bloom" of algae. It was nothing too complicated, but drinking water had to be boiled for a few days until the county decided the algae had reached a safe level.

Inez said that when she traveled to Mexico to see her family, she had gotten into the habit of just drinking bottled water for similar safety reasons. When she came back to the States, she kept on drinking it, so we added "HABIT" to our list.

When we couldn't come up with any more reasons, I showed them my list and said, "There appears to be a bunch of reasons we make these purchases other than immediate necessity." Then I took another tack.

"Jackie, how much was the water?" It had cost her a dollar and fifteen cents.

"And did you complain when you paid it?"

Jackie looked at me quizzically. "No? Why would I complain?"

"I'm just pointing out that you knew free water was available, yet you purchased bottled water with no price objections."

I went on. "And Kirk, you're always complaining about the cost of gas." Kirk drove a car that was so old it surprised us every time it showed up to work. The term "guzzle"' might have been coined for this very automobile. "What's the cost of a gallon of gas?"

Kirk winced, "Two-oh-eight a gallon." I didn't bother asking how they all felt about fuel prices. Gas prices were climbing and everyone hated it. Kirk, Inez and Jackie had all complained about rising fuel costs and put that down as a justifiable reason for pay increases on the next review.

But now I had them, so I asked the important question that brought it all together.

"Let's figure it out. Bottled water is costing you around a dollar a pint. Two pints make a quart, and four quarts make a gallon. So you are paying eight dollars a gallon for **water**, which you could get for free either at home or from the sink here, and, you're not complaining? But gasoline, which has to be drilled from wells, pumped to the surface, refined, shipped around the world, have filling stations built and finally brought to your neighborhood, costs only two dollars a gallon and you're complaining?"

They look at me with mouths open.

"Why don't you complain about the price of bottled water? Water, which from this label appears to be just **spring** water which comes right from the ground anyway, for free? Why do you have a price objection over the cost of gas, while having no objection on the price of something as silly as bottled water which is four times higher?"

I waited, but I knew that one is a puzzler for most people.

Finally, I stated the obvious. "You don't complain because you are making the purchase based on more than immediate necessity. You each have your reasons for making these purchases, and to you they are not just because you 'want a drink of water,' but because, in your minds, you have sufficient data to justify that you truly **need** to purchase bottled water. You've probably even got data on why you need to purchase certain brands of bottled water."

They were thinking. I could see it in their faces. Good.

"Do you think there might be reasons for the products purchased from us beyond the simple fact that the customer has an immediate necessity for vision? Most people wait two to three years before returning to see a doctor and purchasing new eyewear, so I can't believe that everyone is in 'immediate need' of glasses."

That is the same in most retail environments. Little is ever purchased, with the exception of emergency aid or meals, with immediate necessity in mind.

I then gave the members our Fraternity the next lesson, which is the secret of overcoming all price objections ever faced in retail.

Lesson #25 – Price objections are value objections. Anyone will make any purchase at any time, if they perceive that the value is high enough when justified against the purchase price. Price alone means nothing without an attached value - by itself, it's just numbers.

"No way. If that was true then people would be buying everything they see," said Inez.

"I have a hard time believing that, too," said Jackie.

Kirk just shook his head. "Boss, I respect you, but that's not right. You can't make a purchase if you don't have the money."

Kirk brought up a good point, but it was irrelevant to the discussion. He was confusing *funding* with *spending,* a common mistake which often happens to inexperienced people working in sales.

"People who need glasses and have funding are going to make a purchase somewhere, you agree?" I asked and Kirk nodded.

I was pointing out to Kirk a key difference in Tourists, the difference between those who could afford the products, but thought they were too expensive `(price objectors)`, and those who actually couldn't afford the products at all. The latter wasn't a price objection, it was a *financial restriction.*

There's nothing you can do with true financial restrictions except do your best to work within the constraints of available funding.

"But how do you tell the difference? People just say 'that's too much for my budget' and then leave to shop someplace cheaper. What are we supposed to do, argue with them?" Inez wanted to know, as everyone did, if there was a way to separate those with funding restrictions from those with money who were just expressing price objections. "How can you tell the difference?"

"Easy. Listen to the objection. When you hear someone say 'that's too much' or 'I saw that for less somewhere else' or even 'I don't want to pay that much,' it's just smoke - a price objection. They are really telling you they don't yet see the **value** in the product when balanced against the price."

Kirk asked the follow - up, "And what do they say when it's a financial restriction?"

"They say nothing. They just show you their checkbook," I said.

Everyone laughed, but it was true. I pointed out that I am a fairly outgoing individual, and I hold very few secrets. But when it comes to my finances, especially my checkbook ledger, I show nobody.

Kirk was laughing.

"Kirk, do you ever show *your* mother and father the inside of your checkbook?" I asked.

"Heck no! If I did they might stop slipping me money for gas."

That was a dig on me and a reminder about promised pay increases from the upcoming reviews, but I let it pass.

"Inez? You're close with your family. Do you and your dad ever sit down and go through your bills and what you're spending your money on?"

Her head shook no and she looked terrified. "My dad would lecture me for days if he saw how I spent my money."

Jackie was arguing. "I let my mother see my checkbook anytime she wants."

"Don't you and your mother share a checking account?" Kirk asked.

"Shut up, Kirk, that's not the point!" Jackie blurted.

"Ok, then show **us** your check book. Let us look at your balance."

She was getting more upset the more Kirk egged her on, and we all stopped to find out what was wrong.

"I'm broke! OK? There I said it! Next month is my son Rami's birthday, and he wants this *Meg-o-Log©* building kit and I don't even have the money to buy a stupid toy. The balance in my checkbook is five dollars."

I turned to the other two. "There. That's the difference. That's a financial restriction and that's how it sounds."

Let me pause for a second to say that Rami actually got four *Meg-O-Log*© building kits for his birthday that next month. Jackie got the money from her mother to make her purchase; and Inez, Kirk and I each made our own purchases and dropped them off at different times. Rami was thrilled, but we realized that we all better start checking with each other before we continued to make similar duplication mistakes. We didn't ever start checking with each other before shopping for presents, so we still all bought multiple similar gifts for recipients in the future.

Inez brought us back on topic.
"So why do customers try to smoke us?"
"Smoke is what you say to save someone else's feelings and give you an easy out. They don't want to, or can't, express that they haven't seen enough value to make a purchase, so they use a smoke phrase to diffuse the situation," I explained.
"People, whether they think they are or not, are basically socially polite. Have you ever told a kid collecting for Muscular Dystrophy that you gave at the office when they show up at your door at night unexpected?"
Sheepishly, everyone nodded.
"Ok, that's smoke. Saying you gave at the office stops you from saying 'I'm cheap and I'm not going to give you a nickel because I get nothing directly out of it' to a twelve-year old. We use smoke all the time; even when you see an old friend and say 'Hey, we should get together some time' it's usually smoke to politely escape without hurting anyone's feelings."
Kirk was thinking hard.
"But you said, 'Anyone will make any purchase at any time, if they perceive that the **value** is high enough when justified against the purchase price.' That can't be true."
They needed an example of value positively affecting a decision to buy even when money was short, so I gave it to them.

"Let's say I've got a car I want to sell. It's one thousand dollars. Anyone want to buy it?"

Kirk perked right up, "What kind is it?"

"Right!" I almost jumped up I was so excited. "The first thing you want to understand in any purchase is the value of what you're getting in exchange for your money. You know the value of one thousand dollars, it represents probably two weeks of hard work. You don't know the value of the car until I give you some data. Let's say it's a brand new *DMW© M261-c©*."

"That's the convertible!" Inez was excited because in this month's set of sales tools she had tagged the ad for that very car with a Paste-It that said, 'Like driving with the top down? You'll need sunglasses!' and it had generated four new sales from convertible owners.

"Right. Brand new, nothing wrong with it, twenty miles on it and no accidents. I just won the lotto and want something different so I'm selling it for a thousand. Who wants it?"

They all wanted it.

"Now, who's got the money?" They all balked.

"I'll give you a credit card" said Inez.

"What do I look like, a credit card machine. I've only got one slot and you won't want the card back if I swipe it there. Who else?"

Kirk said, "I'll bring you the money tomorrow."

He wasn't getting away that easily, "No. I want to sell it right here, right now."

"Will you take a check?" asked Jackie. She had stopped being upset over her finances so I felt safe to tease her.

"Not from you; I know your balance." And we all laughed.

They were getting inventive now.

"What if we gave you Kirk's car," They were counting hard cash on hand, "one hundred and fourteen dollars, and promised you all of next week's crumb-cake?"

"SOLD!" I shouted and everybody laughed again.

"The point is, even when you don't have cash in your pocket, you have access to funds from somewhere, and you will jump through hoops to make a purchase you see the value in. Now, what if I had said the car was a lime green *Punto©* with two hundred eighty-five thousand miles on it and a bad tranny?"

Nobody wanted it.

"It's all about *perceived value* guys. The objections don't even come up if the perceived value is high enough."

"But they can get the same thing upstairs for less. Isn't that an even better value?"

"Maybe," I said, "If all they know of glasses is some pieces of plastic, glass and wire are put together to make you see and everything is equal. But it's not equal. They can't get the same thing up there, because no matter what they buy up there it comes without a Customer Excellence Advisor, a Strategic Vision Consultant and an Optical Technology Liaison watching over their order. These are skills only available here. Our warrantees are only available here. Our assistance is only available here."

They smiled, they were getting it.

"Now, it will mean more work, but we've got to become experts on everything we sell. Inez, we need to know everything about the lenses we carry and how they compare against the competition. Kirk - frames. We need to know every frames feature and how each of them benefits the customers."

CHAPTER TWENTY-TWO
Overcoming Price Objections

Price objections are like barriers that keep the Guide from completing the Tour; unfortunately they also keep the Tourist from reaching her desired destination. Nobody wins. The Tourist has wasted her time; the Guide has wasted her time and nothing gets accomplished. If the Tourist is seriously interested in getting to the place where her needs are satisfied, then a purchase must be made; otherwise the entire excursion was pointless.

There are nine common sources of price objections. Each is an opportunity to increase or decrease perceived value. Think of them as little rest areas along every Tour. If the little rest areas are positive experiences, the entire Tour proceeds smoothly; miss one, forget to address one or have a bad experience at one, and Tourists may quit before reaching the final destination.

I wrote down what I knew were the top nine objections to perceived value that any retail location faces: ***purpose, identity, influence, look, attitude, presence, support, functionality*** and ***expertise.*** Then we began looking at each separately.

Expertise we had covered. Inez, Kirk and Jackie were committed to making certain every Tour from this moment forward, would be the best possible experience.

Attitude I thought we had down as well. Attitude is all about believing in ourselves, our store, our products and services, and I think we have learned to do that.

Presence is all about branding. Our shop carried plenty of brands, but were we using them correctly? It became apparent looking around the store that we weren't. After the last painting the store looked fresh and open. We had removed anything tired and old, so every piece of point-of-sale advertising had been trashed.

"Contact every vendor we represent and ask them for anything they can send us to promote their products - signs, posters, display, you name it, but let me know the costs before you order anything."

"Check." Jackie was writing.

Presence also helps with **influence**.

"Jackie, how can we expand *influence*?"

"You're losing me." Jackie needed a clarification.

"OK, *influence* is the verb form of *presence*. You know a brand, like *Nipe©* sneakers, the ones with the *swash* symbol?"

Jackie nodded, so I went on.

"When a pro basketball player wears Nipes in a picture, that's *influence*; it reminds the consumers to purchase those sneakers. The more people get influenced, the more likely they are to purchase the sneakers without questioning the cost. How can we build influence in our store?"

Jackie thought then said, "Maybe we could ask the vendors if any of their products are endorsed, and if so, see if they can get us copies of the endorsements like photos, ads or anything else?"

That sounded fine. Kirk and Inez could help contact the vendors and ask for their support. Jackie scribbled a few more notes then dashed off, "I'm on it."

"Kirk, you're in charge of compiling information on our products and making certain we are all fully briefed. There are two areas I really need you to concentrate on: **functionality** and **support**."

Kirk smiled. I liked him for that; he was one of those people who enjoyed being busy and having a project to complete.

"OK, *functionality*. You want to know everything the products do, right?"

"Yeah," I said. "Knowing the features and benefits of something is Sales 101. You didn't need me to teach you that; but *functionality* is more inclusive than just what a product does. We usually know what something can be used for; I also want to know when it can't or shouldn't be used or suggested. I want to know all the product's strengths and its weaknesses. I don't want to be caught off guard if the competition brings up a shortcoming we may have overlooked in anything we offer. So we want to know everything - even what it can't do. That's what I mean by *functionality*."

"Wouldn't that be **DIS**-*functionality*?"

I waited. Kirks eyes finally dropped. I smiled. "Humor me? Just make sure we know everything that something won't do. I want to be prepared to discuss downsides when compared to similar products."

"Can do." Kirk said. "What about *support*?"

"When you're on the phone with the suppliers, tell them we want an up-to-date copy of all warrantees. We're going to post them around the office?"

"Why?" Kirk asked.

"Because often, when people are debating making a purchase they think is too expensive they forget the value of products that come with enforceable guarantees. We can ease their anxiety if we assure them that what they are buying isn't going to fall apart. Also, they like knowing what is covered in case of breakage. That's how we handle *support*."

"Makes sense to me" said Kirk. "I was looking for a place to eat lunch last week, and I stopped in at McDingles. I hardly ever go there but they had a huge sign that said *'Try the new Whipper Super©; if you don't like it - it's free!'* So I tried one."

"How was it?"

"Horrible. The Super doesn't have the fried pickles. Instead they add another beef patty and some pickled beets."

"I know. Did you take it back?"

"No," said Kirk. "It wasn't that big a deal to me, but I never would have tried it without seeing the guarantee."

"What if it had been delicious?"

"Then I would have been back a dozen times already. It's right on my way home. I pass it every day."

"How much was it?"

"About a buck more than then original," Kirk recalled.

"See, promoting *support* through your guarantees works."

By the time they finished their calls the doors were opening. I wanted to get more done but it would wait until the next meeting. The last comment came from Jackie who was really excited.

"They're sending us a bunch of stuff!" she seemed about to burst.

"How much is it going to cost?" I prepared myself for the worst.

"Nothing!" she was bouncing, "They all said they would send everything for free since we're promoting their products!"

"Wow."

It was a long week. The competition hurt us with the sale, and even I felt the pressure.

In football, teams have off years when everyone says, "They are in a re-building period." The next week was our rebuilding period.

Since traffic was slower, we had daily meetings with vendors and suppliers hearing about the latest advances and products we could have. We learned about what products could do, and what they could not do; how they compared to competitive products on the market; and where we had advantages and occasionally disadvantages. We researched prices and became experts on maximizing available discounts and package sales to get the most out of the sales for the Tourists.

By Wednesday, the Point of Sale displays began arriving and by the next Saturday meeting we had so many that we were going to have to make decisions on what was necessary to display, and what we didn't want out.

Every vendor we saw brought us information on warrantees and we were shocked that much of what we sold was guaranteed unconditionally for periods from thirty days to a year.

Saturday finally rolled around and with it the one-year anniversary of the Fraternity of the Retail Guides. We were one month away from the deadline for payroll reviews and I would be damned if I was sending in everyone's reviews after a down month. We had thirty days to show what we could do, or it would all appear to have been a waste in my team's eyes.

To be certain, we all showed up two hours before opening. This would be the last meeting before reviews and we needed to make some last minute, important, changes.

"We're ready," said Kirk.

"Almost," I said. "There still are three areas for value objections you need to know about: **look, purpose** and **identity**. If we can handle those, we are all set."

"First, crumb-cake." And with that Kirk took the aluminum foil off this week's heaven.

"Stop for a second," I said, "and just gaze at this."

It was perfection. It was **always** perfection. It looked like you wanted something delicious to look. The powdered sugar was just right; the crumbles were just right; the way it sat in the pan was just right. It looked totally tempting.

"Anyone want some?" Kirk asked.

We all got some and then discussed the idea of **look**.

"In real estate," I prompted, "It's called *curb appeal*." It means that you need to make something look like it's worth every penny and more. Before they show a house they put flowers in the vases and mow the lawn; they redecorate - anything that will show it off in its best light."

"Like a bride," Inez said with a dreamy far-off look. We waited three seconds, then the rest of us almost fell to the floor laughing.

"A what?" asked Jackie.

"Did she say," and Kirk lifted an arm like a ballerina, "a bride?"

Inez came back down to earth. "Yes, a bride. You know how on a bride's wedding day she gets the special hairdo and the special make-up? Brides do that to look their absolute best because this is the day they want everyone to see them."

Her point was made, but we still didn't know what was up with her moment of fugue state when she mentioned it.

"Ok, I can work with that. The frames are our little "brides" and I want each and every one of them presented to the, ah, "guests" as perfectly beautiful as possible."

For the next half hour we placed sales materials and created displays; we made fashion areas and pasted brands, promo shots and magazine shots near every associated item. We never overdid an area, but we left no doubt about which brands we represented or why they were famous.

Warrantee cards went up, with highlighted guidelines.

When we finished, the store looked more than complete. It looked elegant, informative, imaginative, inviting and fun.

Look was completed. We were left with two areas.

"Inez? What was the deal with brides?" I asked. I thought I knew, but I wanted to hear it.

"Well, I wasn't going to say anything until next month, but Ron proposed."

Ron was her boyfriend of almost four years and we all thought the subject of matrimony seemed to be beyond his repertoire; obviously we were wrong. A round of congratulations went out and we were informed that we all were invited to the wedding in three months.

It was the perfect opening for a discussion on ***identity***.

"Kirk? Jackie? If you hadn't been told just now, how would you have known that Inez sees herself as a bride?"

"I guess we wouldn't," they admitted together.

"That's *identity*; and that's how you work that area. You ask. You talk with people about more than just what they're here to buy. You talk with them about what's going on at their jobs, in their lives, when they're busy and when they're spending free time. You find out who they are by finding out how they see themselves. Then you can recommend products that they are looking for subconsciously, that they might not even know they would prefer."

"Huh?" said Jackie.

Kirk went on, now as Jackie's translator. "Remember when Mrs. Thompson was in?"

A groan went through the room. Mrs. Patsy Jo Thompson was our perpetual shopper. She had spent twenty hours in our shop last month, coming in again and again. She was a very attractive woman in her mid-fifties and always dressed very elegantly, even when she shopped.

But what made her stick out the most was her tendency to wipe off each frame with an alcohol tissue before trying them on - every time. Even if she'd tried them on only seconds earlier.

After her first half dozen visits, everyone had given up on the prospect of making a sale with her, except Kirk. Kirk never gave up and eventually Kirk found her objection, and it was identity.

"You all kept showing her designer sunglass frames that were beautiful, but you missed it."

We remembered, and we laughed and laughed.

We all said it together, "the tattoo."

Kirk had spent the better part of a slow afternoon working with Mrs. Thompson. She had stated that she was looking for a pair of sunglasses in which she would require prescription lenses. As each of us had done time and time again, Kirk presented Mrs. Thompson with options, each being met with the same objections: "These are not right" and "These are a little too pricey." While Kirk seemed worn from the effort, Mrs. Thompson appeared as fresh as the moment she walked in the shop two hours earlier.

Today's ensemble differed from her usual attire in that her usual slacks had been replaced by a beautiful tailored wool skirt that fell just below her knees. The skirt was not tapered, but fell straight with a very small, very appropriate slit of exactly four inches on the side to allow for sitting - probably at a desk, a conference table or a society luncheon.

That slit gave her secret away to Kirk.

As Kirk handed Mrs. Thompson yet another elegant designer frame, similar to the dozens we had all handed her in the past, Mrs. Thompson bent down to pluck a fresh alcohol tissue from her purse on the floor. The skirt rode up an inch, as skirts tend to in this situation. The slit opened slightly, as slits tend to do. And briefly glimpsed by Kirk was Mrs. Thompson's secret, discretely hidden on the outside of her right thigh just above the knee.

We were all laughing hysterically at this point, because we loved how Kirk told this story. We regained composure in anticipation of the punch line we had heard before, but never tired of hearing.

"It was Buddy Holly." And everyone went to the floor in howls of laughter.

It seems that Mrs. Thompson had grown up in Lubbock, Texas. And Buddy Holly's mom and Mrs. Thompson's mom were trying to play matchmaker with their children. They had set the two up, and while socially it never worked out, Mrs. Thompson remained a huge fan of the singer. On the "day the music died," she had got the tattoo as a tribute to a man she had once turned down in the back seat of a car, and ever after turned up on the radio.

"After that it was easy," Kirk stated flatly.

"Because, it was never about price. It was about her *identity*: how she saw herself and how she wanted to see herself when she looked in the mirror," I said in agreement.

"How much was the sale again?" Jackie asked.

"Twenty two hundred dollars," Kirk said. "Six pair total, with four of the six being duplicate pairs of those Buddy Holly sunglasses, all with polarized prescription lenses."

"Guys," I was happy they understood. "It's not always going to be stamped on their face - or on their thigh in this case. You're going to have to dig. Talk to them, listen to them and get to know who they really are."

We had less than five minutes to go before the store opened and one final source of value objections remained for me to explain: **Purpose**.

It was too big a concept, too heavy and too serious, but I did my best.

"*Purpose* is seeing, understanding and respecting 'the big picture.'" I began.

"It goes beyond shopping, sales, service, buying, expertise, attitude and price. It transcends the Guide and the Tourist, surrounding and encompassing everything relating to the Tour."

"To address it demands *scope*, something that usually can't be taught. Guides either have it or they don't."

Kirk was close. "What are you talking about? Like the 'force' in Star Wars?"

"Yes and no. Guys, there's always a bigger picture in life and true Guides get that. Yeah, we're here to sell and they're here to buy, but we are involved in an experience together. We really are on a Tour together, Guide and Tourist. No other Tour will be this Tour. You've got to give it the respect and admiration it deserves because each Tour only happens once."

Jackie and Inez thought I was kidding for a moment.

"You're serious about this, Jeff, aren't you?" Jackie asked.

"I'm serious about every Tour, not just Sales Tours," I offered.

"Over the last few months I have helped each of you along. In a way, I've given you each a Training Tour. I've helped you where I could and guided you along, but *purpose* is something you either have in you to respect and feel, or you don't. I can't teach it to you. You've either got the ability to see beyond the sale, or you don't. If you have it, you'll be amazed how few price objections you'll have."

"Why?" asked Inez.

"Because Tourists can tell; they can tell when you're in it for more than the money. They can tell when it's more than a job or another sale. They can tell when you're really there to help - price be damned. And when they can feel it, they respect it too and objections tend to vanish."

"Wow!" said Kirk.

"Wow!" said Inez.

"Wow!" said Jackie.

"Yeah. it's pretty 'wow,'" I said.

We opened the doors.

EPILOGUE

Two months later I was promoted. The pay increases had been approved, which made sense since we had set a corporate record for "Highest Retail Sales per Square Foot" that last month. Records which, I believe, still stand today.

I'm sure bigger shops have been built since then that have produced much higher gross sales, but not from a postage-stamp store.

That month, of the hundred-plus corporate locations, we beat out shops twenty times bigger and with ten times the employees. My fears were never an issue. All my staff proved themselves great Professional Guides.

But following our success, changes came and it wasn't the same. Why have all the star performers under one roof? My District Manager sent me on to bigger locations and from there to Quality Auditing, and eventually I became a Trainer.

Inez got married and quit, lured by a huge salary offer from the competition.

Jackie had another child and decided that her true calling was a Children's Guide - or parent, if you prefer the standard terminology. I handed it to her; it appears to be one of the most rewarding Guide positions one can aspire to hold.

Kirk ended up leaving too, and joined the military. I received a letter from him once. He told me a story of traveling through an actual Jungle, and how much of what we discussed about Guides and Tours, helped him make it through.

The store was closed several years later. It seems nobody else could make it work. The new Manager, running from the benefit of our sales numbers, started with eleven staff, eight full-time and three part-time, and as sales dwindled he eventually let all but two go. At that point he felt the demands of working the location were too much pressure and quit.

The District Manager never found another Manager willing to put their career on the line for such a small location, so when the lease came up for renewal a decision was made to simply close it down.

But our successes stayed with us, wherever our treks led.

Sales – is not – Simple. Neither is being a Guide. Both require a mix of skills; some that can be cultivated and developed over time, and one or two that simply must be in you to begin with.

If you feel the drive, don't give up. Work each day to make yourself better. And remember, it's all about you, The Guide, and Them, the Tourists, creating the right Tour and having scope of purpose.

Get them through the Jungle safely. Help them find their destinations.

Kirk's Mother's Crumb Cake

We never did get the complete recipe for Kirk's mother's Close to Heaven Crumb-Cake figured out. Years later, in 2007, I read a very similar-looking recipe called "*Big Crumb Coffeecake with Rhubarb*" in the *New York Times*©. It wasn't exactly the same but it was close.

Attached is that recipe with some small changes I've made to bring it closer to the crumb-cake heaven I remember.

It's not perfect though, so feel free to make your own changes as well. I still do - adding here and subtracting there.

We will never know exactly what Kirk's mother added to make her recipe so wonderful, but I have a guess.

She added **purpose**; and she added **love**.

Close to Heaven Crumb-Cake

For the rhubarb filling:
1/2 pound rhubarb, trimmed
1/4 cup sugar
2 teaspoons cornstarch
1/2 teaspoon ground ginger

For the crumbs:
1/3 cup dark brown sugar
1/3 cup granulated sugar
1 teaspoon ground cinnamon
1/2 teaspoon ground ginger
1/8 teaspoon salt
1/2 cup (1 stick or 4 ounces) butter, melted
1-3/4 cups all purpose flour

For the cake:
1/2 cup sour cream
1 large egg
1 large egg yolk

2 tablespoons vanilla
1/2 cup oatmeal
1 cup all purpose flour
1/2 cup sugar
1/2 teaspoon baking soda
1/2 teaspoon baking powder
1/2 teaspoon nutmeg
1/4 teaspoon salt
6 tablespoons softened butter, cut into 8 pieces.

Powdered sugar for top of cake

1. Preheat oven to 325 degrees. Grease an 8-inch-square baking pan with butter. For filling, slice rhubarb 1/2-inch thick and toss with sugar, cornstarch and ginger. Set aside.

2. To make crumbs, in a large bowl, whisk sugars, spices and salt into melted butter until smooth. Then, add flour with a spatula or wooden spoon. It will look and feel like solid dough. Leave it pressed together in the bottom of the bowl and set aside.

3. To prepare cake, in a small bowl, stir together the sour cream, egg, egg yolk and vanilla. Using a mixer fitted with a paddle attachment, mix together flour, oatmeal, sugar, baking soda, baking powder, nutmeg and salt. Add butter and a spoonful of sour cream mixture and mix on medium speed until flour is moistened. Increase speed and beat for 30 seconds. Add remaining sour cream mixture in two batches, beating for 20 seconds after each addition, and scraping down the sides of bowl with a spatula. Scoop out about 1/2 cup batter and set aside.

4. Scrape remaining batter into prepared pan, then spoon rhubarb over batter. Dollop remaining set-aside batter over rhubarb; it does not have to be even.

5. Using your fingers; break topping mixture into crumbs, about 1/2-inch to 3/4-inch in size. Sprinkle over cake. Bake cake until a toothpick inserted into center comes out clean of batter (it might be moist from rhubarb), 45 to 55 minutes. Cool completely before serving.

6. Lightly sprinkle top of cooled cake with powdered sugar before serving.

Makes 1 really big serving (more if other people find out you've made it and demand you share).

CPSIA information can be obtained at www.ICGtesting.com
Printed in the USA
BVOW011102180911

271529BV00007B/1/P